UNDERSTANDING The New Testament

Ralph P. Martin

Acts

A BIBLE STUDY BOOK

SCRIPTURE UNION
47 Marylebone Lane
London W1M 6AX

A. J. HOLMAN COMPANY
division J. B. Lippincott Company
Philadelphia and New York

©1967 Scripture Union
First published 1967
Reprinted April 1967
Reprinted April 1968

Published in Daily Bible Commentary Vol. 3 1974
Reprinted 1977
First published in this edition 1978
Reprinted 1978
ISBN (Scripture Union) 0 85421 611 1

U.S. Library of Congress Cataloging in Publication Data

Martin, Ralph P.
　　Acts: a Bible study book.

　　(Understanding the New Testament)
　　Reprint of the ed. published by Scripture Union, London, issued in series: Bible study books.
　　1. Bible. N.T. Acts—Study—Outlines, syllabi, etc. I. Title. II. Series.

BS2626.M3　　1978　　226'.6'07　　78–9086
ISBN–0–87981–113–7

Printed and bound in Great Britain by
McCorquodale (Newton) Ltd, Newton-le-Willows, Merseyside.

INTRODUCTION

Since their introduction, Scripture Union Bible Study Books have enjoyed wide popularity both in their original paperback and more recently as the hardback Daily Bible Commentary. The continued demand has led to their production in this new format. They are unique in that they can be used both as a daily Bible reading aid and as commentaries for individual or group use.

A Daily Bible Reading Aid

Each volume is divided into sections of an appropriate length for daily use. Normally each volume provides material for one quarter's use, the exceptions being Mark (two months) and 1 and 2 Corinthians and Galatians (four months). Sections have not been dated but where it has been felt appropriate that two be read together in order to complete the book within a quarter they are marked with an asterisk.

New Testament Commentaries

Every major passage is expounded with devotional warmth, clear explanation and relevance to daily life. Most commentaries follow the rather artificial verse divisions, but here the writers have been commissioned to divide the material according to the best exegetical pattern. They thus follow natural units which allow the comments to follow more closely the flow of the original writers' thought.

These commentaries can be used with any Bible translation.

Well Adapted For Group Study

Adult Bible study groups, which meet in homes or elective adult Bible classes of the church school may employ these commentaries with great profit. The Scripture portions are of a length particularly suited to group study.

Acts

INTRODUCTION

Name. Early Christian writers speak of the books of the New Testament as the "Gospel and Apostle". By this description they mean our gospels and the epistles which form the bulk of the New Testament literature. These are understandable groupings, but one further term is needed to explain how the Church came into being, and how the facts of the Gospel history are to be connected to their inspired interpretation in the apostolic letters. This "bridge" book which links the two chief parts together is the Acts of the Apostles.

Purpose. The main purposes of the book of Acts, apart from the obvious provision of a history of the Christian Church in its formative years of growth and development, are as follows:

(*a*) The first aim of the book is to provide a chronicle of the mighty and triumphant progress of the Gospel through the then-known world. This theme is clearly spelled out in Acts **1.8**, and pursued in each chapter of the book. It does not pretend to be a history of all the apostles, nor of the early church in all its parts up to the author's time, nor is it a series of biographical sketches. History and biography are included to serve a larger purpose—namely, to show the universal spread of the Christian faith which was begun and maintained by the Holy Spirit.

Certain emphases are given to spotlight the chief features of the Gospel's advance: the work of Stephen, who first made articulate (in his speech, ch.**7**) the worldwide scope of the message; the actual Gentile message (in ch.**13**), with its antecedents in the conversion of the Ethiopian (ch.**8**); the conversion of Saul (ch.**9**), and the conversion of Cornelius (ch.**10**); and the work of Paul, whose missionary task is implicit in his conversion-call (**9.15**).

(*b*) Another purpose is that which is stated by the author at the frontispiece of his book (**1.1-4**). In both his gospel and the Acts, Luke proposed to supply for Theophilus an accurate and progressive summary of the origins of the Church and its faith, about which he had already received as an interested enquirer some information. Theophilus is evidently neither a proper name nor a fictitious title (meaning "a man dear to God"), but a roundabout way of addressing a representative member of the intelligent middle-class public at

Rome whom Luke wished to win over to a less prejudiced and more favourable opinion of Christianity (so F. F. Bruce).

(c) There is an apologetic intention in this writing which aimed at defending the Christian cause against charges which were popularly brought against it in the latter half of the first century. Luke wants, in this historical narration, to demonstrate that a variety of officials, mainly Roman, bore goodwill to Paul and his friends, and that where they were appealed to and had to settle a dispute between Christians and Jews, there was no substance in the charges levelled at the followers of Jesus. Moreover, Roman military officials show a consistent attitude of interest and sympathy to the Christian message whenever it is presented to them. These factors prove—so Acts demonstrates—that Christianity is politically free from suspicion by the Roman authorities, and this political "innocence" would mean much to a man such as "Theophilus".

Dating. No certainty is possible in arriving at a precise date for the book of Acts, but certain historical factors make it likely that it was first published in the middle of the '60s of the first century. Two events of history in that period are decisively important for the understanding of the Church's life in the world: the persecution of Christians at Rome by Nero (A.D.64), and the outbreak of the Jewish war in A.D.66, which led to the Fall of Jerusalem in A.D.70. The first fact shows that Rome was beginning to be fearful of the Church's influence—a fear enhanced by the overt rebellion of the Jews in Palestine. This would be the opportune time for some statement from a Christian writer that showed that believers in Jesus, unlike the Jews, were not disloyal to the empire. The Acts provides just such a clear statement.

The omission of Paul's martyrdom in A.D.66-68 may be taken to indicate that Luke did not know of it when he wrote; and this may fix the date of the book as *after* A.D.64 and *before* A.D.66-68.

Writer. Early Church tradition associates the author of both gospel and Acts with Luke, the doctor of Colossians 4.14, and the "companion of Paul" (Irenaeus). The attestation which couples Luke's name with the book of Acts is both early (the first mention is given in the anti-Marcionite prologue to the third gospel, c.A.D.160-180) and widespread (including the Church Fathers from Irenaeus to Jerome).

The evidence from the book of Acts itself amply endorses this tradition, and there are clear indications that the author was the same as the man who composed the third gospel and was an associate of Paul.

Historical accuracy. Provided we do not ask from the book what it was never intended to give—*viz.,* a comprehensive and detailed account of the social origins of Christianity, we may have every confidence in the author's painstaking interest in securing a reliable record. Indeed, this is exactly the claim he makes for himself (Lk.**1.**3, R.S.V. marg.); and scholars like E. Meyer, Sir William Ramsay, F. F. Bruce, and E. M. Blaiklock have pointed to Luke's competence and accuracy in correctly reporting the proper official terms by which Roman governmental personnel were known in the first-century world. Thus *proconsul* and *procurator* are carefully distinguished, and this accurate usage suggests that Luke had first-hand knowledge and was concerned to make a careful investigation of his facts.

Helps. There are books on Acts to suit every need and taste. Historical allusions and much background material are given in E. M. Blaiklock's Tyndale Commentary (I.V.F./Eerdmans) and (with more devotional emphasis) William Barclay's *Daily Study Bible.* Larger works are those by F. F. Bruce (New London/International Commentary), and C. S. C. Williams (Black's N. T. Commentaries). An older commentary by J. A. Findlay has been used in our notes, to much profit.

Note. An occasional reference to the "Western text" of Acts in the pages which follow draws attention to this interesting fifth-century Greek manuscript (*Codex Bezae*) which represents the Western tradition. It has a number of unusual additions, some of them highly imaginative and colourful and possibly authentic.

Acts 1. 1—14

Vs. 1–5 connect Luke's account of how the Good News was brought from Jerusalem to Rome with his earlier record of how the Good News began, set out in his Gospel. The climax of that record was Jesus' resurrection and appearance to His apostles (3), followed by a warning and a promise (4, 5). Is this "baptism with the Holy Spirit" the same as that referred to in 1 Cor. **12.** 13—*i.e.*, marking our entry into the fellowship of the Church?

Vs. 6–11: The apostles are still bemuddled over the meaning of the kingdom (3) and the nature of their task (6, 7); and thoughts of an earthly reign fill their minds (see Mark **10.** 35—45). Jesus directs them to their immediate responsibility (8; what is it? Does it fulfil Isa. **43.** 10?). They must leave the future in God's hands, and attend to what He commissions them to be and do. This missionary task depends upon (*i*) the Lord's ascension (John **16.**5—11; Eph. **4.**8—13); (*ii*) the consequent gift and empowering of the Spirit (Acts **2.** 33 makes this clear, doesn't it?); and (*iii*) the sovereign purpose of God for His

Son in His world (Psa. **2.** 6—8)—a purpose to be completed at His return (11).

Vs. 12-14 show how the apostles interpreted the command to wait (4). What was their chief occupation? The upper room, often identified with the scene of the Last Supper, was to be a hallowed spot, and not least because Jesus had bound these men and women together in love and deep friendship. Even a former tax collector and a nationalist Zealot lost their traditional hatred for each other (13, who are they?) *Notes:* V. 4: "while staying with them" is literally "sharing a meal with them"; *cf.* Luke **24.** 41—43; John **21.** 12—14; Acts **10.** 41, one of the many proofs of His true resurrection. V. 8: the ground plan of the entire book. V. 9: the cloud is an O.T. sign of God's presence. He is received into His immediate presence (John **17.** 11, 24). Questions of how far is "up" are beside the point if God is omnipresent. The Ascension is the withdrawal of Jesus from our earth-bound vision, but not from our world (Matt. **28.** 20). V. 12: 1000 yards are the extent of such a journey. V. 14: the women are those who were last at the cross (Mark **15.** 40, 47) and first at the tomb (Mark **16.** 1, 2).

Acts 1.15-26

Vs. 15-22 give the substance of Peter's statement, addressed to the first problem which faced the infant community. What anticipations can you find of Peter's leadership, in the Gospels? See Matt. **16.**17-19; Mk. **16.**7. The defection of Judas is described in Matt. **27.** 3-10 and should be read in the light of (*i*) his privileged position (17); (*ii*) the fulfilment of Scripture (16,20, quoting Psa. **69.** 25, **109.** 8); (*iii*) his infamous (16), yet self-willed treachery (25); (*iv*) the problem of a successor, created by his death (20b). This much is clear, but the character of Judas remains an enigma and a warning to us; and Scripture refuses to satisfy our curiosity as to his motivation, or to resolve the tension between Divine foreknowledge (John **6.**70,71; **13.**18, **17.** 12) and human responsibility (Mk. **14.**10; John **13.**27; **19.** 11). See I.V.F. *New Bible Dictionary*, "Judas".

Vs. 23-26. Before the matter of a twelfth apostle is settled, some qualifications of the candidates are mentioned (21, 22). What are they? Two are important: (*i*) they must be well-known members of the apostolic band, associated with them during the ministry of Jesus; (*ii*) they must be witnesses *to* (R.S.V.) His resurrection. Why are these features necessary? *Cf.* Luke **1.**2; 1 Cor. **9.**1. Barsabbas and Matthias are nominated; and after prayer for God's guidance, the latter is chosen by the ancient practice of lot-casting (26). Was this the right method of making a selection? What is the significance of the fact that the use of the lot is never repeated after Pentecost, and that Matthias is never heard of again in Acts?

Notes: V. 17: the terms which Peter uses are intended to show a parallel with the election of Matthias. "Judas was numbered with us": God later added to the eleven (making again twelve of them). Judas was allotted a share in the apostles' ministry: his successor was chosen by lot. V. 25: perhaps the saddest and most revealing verdict on Judas. He "turned aside, to go to his own place"—*i.e.*, the place he had chosen for himself. And God confirmed him in that dreadful choice. "Then I saw that there was a way to Hell even from the gates of Heaven, as well as from the City of Destruction" (Bunyan's *Pilgrim's Progress*).

Acts 2.1-13

Vs. 1–4. Originally a festival marking the beginning of the wheat harvest in ancient Israel (Ex. **34.**22), the feast of Weeks was so called because it fell on the fiftieth day after Passover (see Lev. **23.**15*ff.* for the calculation). Hence the term "Pentecost", which means 'fiftieth' in Greek. It is interesting that the later Jews celebrated the giving of the Law at Sinai at this festival, and thought of the voice of God sounding in every nation under heaven. Is this in the background of vs. 6–8?

The disciples were gathered possibly in the Temple precincts or in the upper room when the promise of **1.**4, 8 was made good. There were two outward manifestations of the Spirit's presence and power (2, 3) —notice the guarded language, half concealing exactly what occurred. But the consequentials were unmistakable in Spirit-inspired utterances (4). Christianity lives by the communication of the truth of God to men by men.

Vs. 5-11. What was it that arrested attention among the motley crowd assembled in Jerusalem for the feast? Was it the universality of the Christians' message, each man hearing a language he could understand, although the hearers came from many parts of the ancient world of the Jewish dispersion and the speakers were Galileans who were noted for their guttural accent (Mark **14.**70)? If so, Pentecost witnesses the reversal of Babel (Gen. **11.**1-9). Otherwise, was it the remarkable speech of the disciples which expressed with rapture "the mighty works of God" (11)? This Pentecostal *glossolalia* is apparently different from the spiritual gift in 1 Corinthians **14** (which is to be used in private and public worship, and with caution and restraint).

Acts 2.14-28

Vs. 14-21. The secret of early Christian testimony to "the mighty works of God" (11) is the Spirit, giving them an exuberance and confidence which was mistaken for drunkenness (13; *cf.* Eph. **5.**18). And the Holy Spirit's presence and power are traced to the fulfilment of O.T. prophecy (16): "This is that which was spoken by the prophet Joel". This citation from the O.T. underlines a number of basic apostolic convictions:

(*i*) the Church is living in a new era of God's dealings with men, following directly upon the Cross and triumph of Jesus. These are "the last days" (17: Heb. **1.**1-2 is the best commentary on this phrase); (*ii*) the work of the Holy Spirit, restricted in the O.T. to special persons, is now enlarged to include *all* believers in Jesus as the Messiah (17,18); (*iii*) the Messianic age is often referred to in Jewish literature as the time of God's "salvation" (21). Peter goes on to declare that that promised time has arrived. The age-to-come has come! See 1 Cor. **10.**11.

Vs. 22-28. Peter goes to the heart of the matter by showing how the life, death, and resurrection of Jesus of Nazareth have inaugurated this new chapter in God's relations with the world. We must mark again some vital emphases of Christian conviction: (*i*) Jesus' ministry was that of 'a Man appointed by God'—*i.e.*, Messianic (22); (*ii*) His death at the hands of the Romans was no accident, but part of God's age-old plan (23); (*iii*) Peter's reference to Psalm **16** (25-28) illustrates again the use of O.T. "testimonies"—*i.e.*, Scripture passages which point to the Age of the Messiah, now begun. Paul will use the same thought in a later sermon (**13.**33*ff.*)

Notes: V. 15: "third hour" = 9 a.m.; and on that day a fast was observed until mid-morning. V. 17: the promised Spirit comes on all, irrespective of class and sex (Gal. 3.14,28; 1 Cor. **12.**12,13). V. 21: the key word is "saved", but given here a richer meaning than in Joel **2.**28*ff.* V. 22: a reference to Jesus' Galilean ministry, evidently known in Jerusalem. V. 24: read "snares set by death".

To think over: What criterion decides the literal (27) and non-literal (19,20) fulfilment of prophecy?

Acts 2.29-36

We may take these verses as a single unit. They form the third and concluding part of Peter's Pentecostal address, and follow the earlier pattern—namely, a personal address (14,22) to his hearers (29:

"Brethren"); a statement of Christian conviction (29-33); and an O.T. quotation which buttresses that affirmation (34,35). Note the *extra* feature in this final section (36).

The allusion to Psalm **16** is now explained. Though written by David, it cannot refer only to him because he died (29: note the sombre finality of "and was buried"—a phrase which belongs also to the earliest Christian creed of 1 Cor. **15.**3*ff.*). His psalm, however, expresses the confidence that this will not happen to God's anointed King, whom David typified. The only possible conclusion, then, is that David was speaking prophetically of the Messiah (30,31). He died—but, when men had done their worst, was vindicated by God in the resurrection.

Three proofs are supplied of the reality of His resurrection here: (*i*) only a bodily resurrection of Messiah can make sense of prophetic Scripture: (*ii*) the apostles themselves are living witnesses to His personal victory over death (see especially the strong statement of Acts **10.**41 in the light of v.32): and (*iii*) only the exaltation of the living Christ can satisfactorily explain the phenomena which his hearers have seen and heard (33). John **14.**16; **16.**7 should now be read.

The mention of the Lord's exaltation requires justification; and Peter finds this in Psalm **110.**1. The dialogue is between God (in His O.T. name, the Lord = Yahweh) and His anointed. David prefigured the Messiah (so all Jews and Christians believe; 2 Sam. **7.**12-14), but David never ascended to heaven. He must, therefore, again have been speaking of the Messiah, "great David's greater Son" (34,35).

The conclusion is irresistible (36). As Jesus of Nazareth alone fulfils both Psalms, He is the true Messiah Who is now installed in the place of honour. His Messiahship, once concealed, is now displayed; and His title to worship, as Lord, is proved (Rom. **1.**3, 4; Phil. **2.**9-11).

Meditation: *The head that once was crowned with thorns*
Is crowned with glory now.

Acts 2.37-47

Vs. 37-42. On that day about three thousand persons entered the fellowship of the Church through the gateway of repentance, forgiveness, and faith, expressed outwardly by baptism and inwardly by the gift of the Holy Spirit (Rom. **8.**16; 1 Cor. **12.**3). St. Augustine, in a memorable phrase, described this day as the Church's *dies natalis*, or birthday. Those who were thus introduced to the saving benefits of the Gospel remained in close association (42). Conversion was for them no flash in the pan, or ephemeral, emotional upsurge of religious excitement. Having begun the Christian life, they continued—and doubtless made good progress. Which of the Pauline churches does this remind you of? So unlike the Galatian Christians (Gal. **1.**6; **3.**3,4; **5.**7).

Vs. 43-47 are verses which paint a cameo picture of the first Christian fellowship. Note who the leaders were (43). And how the "common life in the body of Christ" was expressed, both in social responsibility (44,45) and spiritual exercises (46). It is a travesty to set these against each other as mutually exclusive. Right at the beginning of the Gospel age, in a Church fellowship which had come straight from the Lord's hands, there was a "holy worldliness" *and* a "sacred worship" in the Temple. Both were important—and still are today! Let us notice too the spirit which prevailed (47a) and the popularity of the young movement (47b), with "a conquering new-born joy" suffusing it all.

Notes: V. 38: baptism "in the Name of Jesus Christ" means a calling on His Name (Acts **22.**16) or, possibly, a claiming of the new believers for Him Who henceforth "possessed" them as their Lord (Acts **10.**48). Faith in Christ is implicit in both meanings, leading to forgiveness and incorporation into the Holy Spirit (1 Cor. **12.**13). V. 39: allusions are made to Isa. **57.**19 and Joel **2.**32 to stress the inclusiveness of the appeal. The Gentiles will eventually be evangelized. V. 42: four aspects of church life are mentioned: "teaching"—a ministry of instruction; "fellowship"—like our church or parochial meeting; "breaking of bread"—a common meal, called later the *agape* (1 Cor. **11.**20,21,33, 34; Jude 12), with which was joined a remembrance of the Lord in His death; "the prayers"—the definite article shows that believers observed the Temple worship. V. 46: the common meal again, practised in the people's homes.

Acts 3.1-10

Acts **2.**43 speaks of the apostles' "wonders and signs", wrought in proof of the divine reality of the Christians' claim to be the people of God. This section gives one illustration of what is meant; and contains a directory of evangelistic "method" which all Christians may profitably study. Luke's purpose, however, in recording the incident, is to indicate the important consequences which followed, leading to a rupture of the Church with Judaism, as Jesus had foreseen (Mark **2.** 21,22).

The scene is laid at the Nicanor gate of the Jerusalem Temple, specially noted for its magnificence. Hence the title, Beautiful Gate. The impotent beggar is a picture of dire need, whose only virtue is an awareness of his sad condition. Peter's response is twofold, in what he said (4,6) and no less important, in what he did (7). The action of the Gospel matches the word of the Gospel; and this is ever the pattern of meaningful evangelism.

The need is met (7) as the Name of Jesus Christ is invoked to release the power which attended His healing ministry in Galilee. So it is seen that the once crucified Jesus is alive, not only as an affirmation of faith or a statement of personal testimony (given in 2.32), but as a dynamic force at work in this world and effective in transforming the lives of those who call upon Him. Similarly, the apostolic message which may have seemed to be so much talk is invested with a new significance. Peter speaks "in the name of Jesus Christ"—and miracles happen. *Cf.* 1 Thess. **1.5**, where the miracle-working accompaniment of Paul's preaching was more in terms of a dedicated group of men than spectacular happenings as in this story. But is the "age of miracles" past?

Notes: V. 1: the Jews observed two hours of daily prayer. The "evening" one was at 3 p.m. V. 2: the Jewish historian Josephus describes this Temple gate as one that "far exceeded in value those gates that were plated with silver and set in gold." V. 6: what could not be bought with money is freely offered. The same phrase in 1 Pet. **1.**18, however, may point to a deeper meaning. Judaism was powerless to meet the beggar's case; the Gospel is able. V. 8: a fulfilment of Isa. **35.**6 and a sign that the Messianic age has arrived, according to Matt. **11.** 4-6. V. 10: there was no mistaking the identity, and so no possibility of explaining away the miracle.

Acts 3.11-16

The sequel to "a notable sign" (**4.**16) gives Peter a chance to improve the occasion with a speech which, in this passage, explains the reason for this event. Disclaiming all personal-kudos (12), he attributes all the glory to God. More specifically, the grounds of the miracle are (*i*) God's purpose in glorifying His servant Jesus (13); (*ii*) the efficacy of Jesus' Name, when invoked by His people and trusted by those in need; and (*iii*) the presence of human faith (16, R.S.V. is certainly helpful here, in what is at best a difficult verse).

This short section is rich in its teaching on God and His purposes in Christ. There is no disparity between God's revelation in both O.T. and N.T. He is still "the God of Abraham, and of Isaac, and of Jacob" to the N.T. writers as to our Lord (Mark **12. 26**). The person of Jesus is described in terms of Isaiah's picture of the suffering servant (**52.13—53.**12), once humiliated but now exalted (Isa. **52.13** in the Greek O.T. uses the same word as v.13). His other titles bear witness to His blameless character, and have parallels in O.T. and in the Inter-Testamental literature which expected a Deliverer for Israel. A more obscure title is "the Author of life" (15) which is found again in Heb. **2.**10, which may suggest His eternal existence (as in John **5.**26) or His ability to grant eternal life to His people (as in 1 John **5.**11,12). Either way it is an expressive term, betraying a high estimate of His person; and in a paradox shows the wonder of His resurrection victory. "You killed Him"—although He was the pioneer of life: "but God brought Him back from death" (15). And He is still at work in healing the lame man.

Notes: V. 11: Solomon's colonnade lay to the east of the outer court, or court of the Gentiles, of the Temple. V. 12: "stare", a different word from that in v.4. V. 13: a liturgical description of God, current in Temple and synagogue worship. Possibly Peter had been reminded of it during the service. V. 13: "Servant", admittedly the Greek word could mean "child" (as R.S.V. marg.), but the reference to Isa. **52—53** seems clear. V. 16: a verse which in its obscurity shows that it is a translation from Peter's original Aramaic language. "Prince of life" in v.15 can equally mean in Aramaic "Prince of salvation", which includes both bodily health and spiritual renewal.

Acts 3.17-26

Peter addresses his Jewish hearers as (*i*) those responsible, through their human leaders, for the Messiah's death (17); and (*ii*) men who could be forgiven, because they acted in ignorance, if they reversed their attitude to Jesus (19), and could be included in the scope of God's saving purpose for Israel (20), declared first to their forefather Abraham (25,26).

Old Testament prophecy is again appealed to in order to show that the Cross was part of a divine plan (18), and also that God's offer in sending Israel's Messiah, likened in v.22 to a second Moses, is not to be trifled with (23). Indeed it is not simply that there are individual prophecies of His coming: the entire fabric of O.T. Scripture is a preparation for the events which have recently taken place, Peter declares (24).

God's redeeming purpose began with Abraham whose family is blessed in succeeding generations (25). Ultimately, as Paul shows in Galatians, this promise will embrace the Gentiles (Gal. 3.6-9,29). But both apostles agree that the offer of Messianic salvation is sent "to the Jew first" (Rom. 1.16: v. 26). This fact stamps all missionary work among the Jewish people with an importance which is unique.

Notes: V. 17: a reference to Luke 23.34 seems intended. Who else "acted ignorantly in unbelief" (1 Tim. 1.13)? Vs. 19,20: "times of refreshing" and the "establishing (of) all that God spoke by the mouth of His holy prophets" go together, and relate to the full joys of the Messianic era, to be consummated at the return of Christ (20). V. 22: John's Gospel enshrines references to this aspect of the Messianic hope, current among the Samaritans who awaited a "restorer" (John 4.19,25,29). V. 26: The verb speaks of Jesus' mission, not His resurrection. He is God's Servant as in Isaiah's prophecy. Just possibly He may be likened to Isaac (25) whose "binding" (Gen. 22) was understood by the Rabbis as atoning for sin.

Questions: In relation to vs. 19,20: (i) Does this section belong particularly to Israel in the future, as in Rom. 11.26-28? (ii) Did Peter expect that His return would occur in the near future, as v. 20 seems to mean? (iii) If "establishing" is translated "restoration" of all things (so R.V.), the thought of cosmic renewal and the renovation of Nature (Rom. 8.18-23; 2 Pet. 3.8-13) may be in mind. Is this the same as Matt. 19.28?

Acts 4.1-12

Such an offer as 3.26 contains seemed too good to be true. It gave the Jews a "second chance" and opened the door to God's Messianic salvation. Many entered in (4). But the Jewish leaders were disturbed (2). Note what it was in the apostles' preaching which upset them most (2). The Athenians found this also hard to accept (17.32); and it is still a rock of offence to modern minds.

The description, "a good deed", is not boastfully made, for Peter's explanation makes it clear that the risen Jesus is the Agent of healing (clearly in v.10). Peter has thrown down the challenge to the Jewish religious leaders in an unmistakable way: Jesus is the Christ, and the Author of Messianic blessedness. The "good time coming", yearned for by prophets and seers, has come in Him. By His death and resurrection God has visited His people with His grace; and has reversed the verdict of those who cried, "Away with Him" (Luke 23.18), prompted by the evil designs and accusations of their leaders (Mark 15.11). Peter's vivid illustration of this reversal (11) would not be lost on those who remembered Jesus' own teaching (Mark 12.10*f.*)

Notes: V. 1: "captain of the temple" means probably police official in charge of the soldiers who guarded the outer court and prevented Gentiles from crossing into the sacred (inner) enclosure. The Sadducees formed a Jewish party of aristocratic priestly leaders. They held a commanding place in the Temple's hierarchy and also in the governing body of legislature, the Sanhedrin. Conservative in belief, they objected to the doctrine of the resurrection (see Mark 12.18). Hence their twofold opposition to the apostolic ministry in the Temple courts. V. 6: Annas was in fact the ex-high priest, but he continued to exert a considerable influence through his son-in-law Caiaphas (Luke 3.2). An important manuscript tradition (the Western text) gives Jonathan for John here. If this is correct, it refers to Jonathan, Annas' son, who succeeded Caiaphas as high priest in A.D.36. Alexander is otherwise unknown to us. V. 7: the two terms "power" (Gk. *dynamis*) and "name" characterize the Church's early days. The apostles were powerful in word and work because they invoked a mighty Name (12: "name" carries its Biblical sense of "revealed character", the person known to others. *Cf.* Ex. 34.5*ff.*). V. 11: the "stoneship" of Christ derives from Ps. 118.22 and is found in Rom. 9.33; Eph. 2.20; 1 Pet. 2.6,7.

Acts 4.13-22

"Enchanted but not changed" is a title of one of Oswald Chambers' studies, and the same description applies here. The leaders were impressed by the apostles' (*i*) boldness of speech, which they could not explain in view of their lack of Rabbinical training; and (*ii*) likeness to Jesus Himself Who was for them no figure of the past but a personal presence Whose spirit they had caught. He also had no formal Rabbinical education (John 7.15).

But that was as far as it went. Reduced to silence by the incontrovertible evidence standing by (Luke's gentle irony), yet unwilling to accept the logical consequence of the miracle and its significance (16), they rather tamely tried to quash the whole matter by muzzling the apostles (18). Men with a crusading and missionary zeal like Peter's and John's will never go meekly home and forget all about it! So they press home the unwelcome logic of vs. 19,20. And further threats do not move them, either (21).

Notes: V. 13: the Greek word means "forthright public speech"; for such a gift Paul prayed in Col. 4.3,4 and Eph. 6.19,20. Many a Christian preacher may very well emulate this, especially when the temptation to compromise or water-down the truth of God is strong. Commentators draw the parallel with Mark 14.67. "A servant-maid of Caiaphas recognizes Peter has been with Jesus because of his overwrought condition; her master comes to the same conclusion for a precisely opposite reason" (Findlay). V. 16: the miracle was common knowledge in the city and no-one could deny it. At a deeper level, the failure of the authorities to challenge the apostles' preaching of Jesus' bodily resurrection is of tremendous interest. "The silence of the Jews is as significant as the speech of the Christians." Why did they not produce the remains of His buried corpse, and silence the apostles for ever? The alleged mythical origins of Christianity as a slowly growing legend, wrapt in obscurity, and a hole-in-the-corner affair are frankly incredible. See Acts 26.26; 2 Peter 1.16. V. 17: how did Luke know what the Council said? The answer may lie in Acts 6.7; or 26.10; or through Gamaliel to Saul of Tarsus, 22.3. V. 19: "listen to" has the common O.T. meaning of "obey" (see Deut. 6.4). Socrates gave an almost identical reply to his accusers. The freedom of the conscience is a foundation-stone of all morality. The tragedy is that over-zealous religious folk often deny it to those from whom they differ. V. 22: his age shows that he was a responsible witness (*cf.* John 9.21).

Acts 4.23-31

The Church which meets us in the pages of the N.T. is a worshipping and witnessing community of believing men and women. The passage in these verses gives a notable example of corporate prayer, offered by the church as it welcomed back the apostles from their interrogation by the Jewish Council (23). The same verb, translated "reported", is found at 14.27 at the close of the first missionary journey. What was the church's reaction then?

Three thoughts are suggested by the record of this earnest petition: (*i*) its Scriptural language (24-26) both in the invocation of God as Creator of the world and (therefore) in control of human destiny, and in the citation of Psalm 2. The fulfilment of this ancient text is seen in the recent events which had brought Jesus to His cross (27), and incidentally stirred up the hostility of the authorities to the first preaching of the message. Yet Christians took comfort from the fact that all these events were under Divine control (28). There may be incidents in the Church's struggle and hardships; but there are no accidents. Rom. **8.**28 is still the great sheet-anchor of faith.

(*ii*) The specific request which the Church voiced (29,30) is related to the need of the hour. Some people find difficulty in justifying this type of prayer by suggesting that God is not interested in our trivial needs. Paul, however, found no such objection: see Phil. **4.**6.

(*iii*) A spectacular consequence followed (31) as the Hearer of prayer answered the need with the Holy Spirit's presence and strengthening power. The very thing they asked for (29) God gave— as Jesus had promised (John **14.**13,14).

Notes: V. 23: Christian footsteps knew the way back to their friends. V. 24: to the R.S.V. refs. add Neh. **9.**6; Isa. **42.**5; Jer. **32.**17 (especially). V. 25: Psalm **2** was one of the Messianic passages in current use (especially Ps. **2.**7). It is quoted again at the Lord's baptism (Mark **1.**11) in conjunction with Isa. **42.**1—a "servant" passage. Vs. 27,30 also connect Jesus with the Servant of God. His "Christhood" (27: "thou didst anoint") is that of God's obedient Servant and royal Son, destined to have universal dominion.

Acts 4.32-37

This is another summary of what life was like for the earliest Christian company. Body, mind, and spirit were involved. For the first, there was a pooling of material resources. Was this a good thing, do you suppose, involving as it did the liquidation of capital assets (34,37)? And was it the cause of the poverty of the Jerusalem church in later years (Acts **11.**29: 2 Cor. **8,**9)? Luke is content simply to report the facts as a proof of Christian concern for the well-being of all, at least for the immediate future, and as a lesson in generosity.

The unanimity of the church is marvellously portrayed in the words "of one heart and soul" (32), fulfilling Jer. **32.**39. And this oneness of mind is the more striking in view of the growth of the church. The term "company" is literally "the multitude" (R.V.), an evidence of the rapid expansion of the Gospel's influence.

On a spiritual level, v. 33 testifies to the effectiveness of their ministry. Note again the central doctrine in the preaching and witnessing. Is it prominent in the Church's proclamation today?

Joseph or Barnabas, a Levite from Cyprus, is picked out for special mention. He is related to John Mark (Col. **4**.10); and Acts **12**.12 may indicate the family connection in Jerusalem where he owned some land. He sold this estate, and turning the asset into money, brought the purchase-price as a gift to the common fund. By this introduction the way is prepared for the later part which he will play in the missionary outreach of the Church (Acts **9**.27; **13**.2).

Looking back over this section, we may ask one or two questions, to which no settled answer is possible, but which provoke our thinking. Was it an expectation of the Lord's near return which motivated the selling of land and houses—and perhaps therefore the teaching to the Thessalonians (2 Thess. **2**.2; **3**.6-13; 1 Thess. **5**.1*ff*.) was a needed corrective? What were the specific aids to Christian unity which these believers used? Fellowship in prayer and service; an agreed gospel message and apostolic teaching; a common meal, at which their unity was symbolically expressed (1 Cor. **10**.17)? *How* did the apostles give their testimony (33)?

Notes: V. 36: Barnabas' name means strictly speaking "son of Nebo" = son of the prophet. The Greek term for "prophecy", however, includes encouragement (1 Cor. **14**.3).

Acts 5.1-11

Just as the idyllic setting of the first man was destroyed by sin's presence, and its effect in Cain's crime, so the fair beauty of the church's life was spoiled by unworthy members. Their sin lay not in keeping back part of their proceeds (as v.4 makes clear), but in trying to deceive others (and God!) that they were in fact more generous than they were. They pretended to give all—the full price of their property—but they had kept back a portion for their own use (2, 8). Their sin was one of vain pretension and hypocrisy; their unholy motive was discerned by Peter (4) whose stern verdict (4b) had a startling effect (5). Peter is no less severe with Sapphira, although he does give her a chance to confess and put things right (8).

"To our minds the whole tone of the story seems un-Christian." So one commentator passes his judgment of this passage, while others find it "frankly repulsive". How would you justify Peter's severe actions? Indeed, how would any of us escape, if our hidden motives and secret sins were laid bare and openly punished (Psalm **130**.3)?

Certain features should be kept in mind in interpreting this passage: (*i*) peculiar significance attaches to this sin because it is the *first* recorded offence in the "new creation"; (*ii*) these early days of Church history were charged with a vivid awareness of God's presence.

Ananias and Sapphira really *believed* what Peter said; and reaped an immediate harvest of their deed (Gal. **6.**7); (*iii*) Paul's teaching is that there is something worse than physical death which may be a chastening experience to bring the soul to its true repentance (1 Cor. **5.**5; **11.** 30-32; 1 Tim. **1.**20); (*iv*) Church discipline meant far more in the early Church than it does to us today. It may be significant that the word "church" occurs for the first time in Acts at verse 11.

Notes: V. 3: this explains the gravity of Ananias' act (*cf.* 4, 9). V. 6: these young men may have been public buriers (like undertakers' assistants today). *Cf.* Ezek. **39.** 12-16.

Acts 5.12-21a

Vs. 12-16. God accredited the apostles as His true servants by accompanying gifts of power and healing miracles. Paul later claimed the same credentials (Rom. **15.**19; 2 Cor. **12.**12). Some suggest that these miraculous powers served a limited function (*i.e.*, to accredit the apostolic Gospel) and were then withdrawn, as B. B. Warfield taught. For others, they are an available accompaniment of the Gospel preaching in every age.

V. 13 is a puzzle, as it stands; and it is not easy to connect the popularity of the young movement with the statement that "none of the rest dared join them." The last verb may carry the sense, "meddle, interfere"; and some scholars wish, with a slight alteration, to read "Levites" for "the rest": "but no one of the Levites dared to interfere with them" by preventing them from holding their meetings in the Temple courts. But the text may mean simply that, in spite of the believers' popularity with the people, those who were attracted to them hesitated to join them because of the judgment-power on insincere motives and hidden sins (exemplified in the case of Ananias and Sapphira). But it must be conceded that verse 14 hardly reads as a natural sequel to this thought.

Vs. 17-21 report another outburst of opposition from official Jewry. The Sadducees (as at **4.**1,2) are again the active fomenters of trouble. Why was it that this Jewish party was stirred to hostility?

Notes: V. 12: see **3.**11 for this part of the Temple: a spot hallowed by Jesus' earlier ministry (John **10.**23). V. 14: *cf.* **2.**47. V. 15: "pallets", like the one used in the story of Mark **2.**4*ff.* V. 15: Peter's healing shadow is not a piece of superstition or magic. Luke doesn't actually say that the apostle's shadow healed, but that the people associated with it the presence of a man of God and, therefore, God's presence.

Cf. **19**.12. V. 17: the phrase sums up the composition (along with the Pharisees, in verse 34) of the Sanhedrin, the Jewish legislature. V. 19: angelic deliverance of this sort will be more fully described in **12.**7*ff*. Paul, too, was released from prison in remarkable circumstances (**16.**25*ff*.). V. 20: "life" and "salvation" both translate the same Aramaic word.

To think over: Do we remember in prayer enough those imprisoned contemporary Christian leaders for whom there is no supernatural release?

Acts 5.21b-32

Vs. 21b-26. The Sanhedrin had evidently expected a full arraignment of the apostles, and a summons to bring them out for trial was issued (21). To the dismay of their foes and captors, the apostles had disappeared and could not be traced anywhere—until it became all too apparent that they had not fled into safe hiding, nor slunk away in abject fear, but were to be found and heard in a public place (25). There is gentle irony here, as Luke records the reactions of those concerned.

Vs. 27-32 give both the command to desist from preaching and the reply that Peter's conscience found this injunction intolerable. The accusation which the high priest makes reminds us of what the Jews said in Matt. **27.**25, and shows how widespread the Gospel's influence was becoming, much to the consternation of the Jewish leaders who saw their own place being undermined. We may recall a similar fear about the effect of Jesus' ministry (John **11.**48).

The brave response of Peter, again spokesman for the rest, in the face of such a threat, is quite in character—that is, in line with the new Peter, who has shed his pre-Easter cowardice and has received a baptism of the Spirit's courage and strength. He repeats his earlier affirmation of loyalty to God (**4.**19); and proceeds to give the urgent reason why his voice cannot be silenced.

The story of Jesus is told again in its impressive simplicity: "God sent Him to Israel as their Messiah; the Jewish leaders rejected Him and engineered His crucifixion; God stepped in, and reversed this judgment of condemnation by raising Him from the dead and installing Him as a life-giving Saviour; we are the eyewitnesses of these facts under the guidance and empowering of the Holy Spirit." How succinct and compelling is this statement! Note the effect it had.

Notes: V. 21b: the "and" explains what follows. Translate "the Council, that is, all the senate." V. 28: the high priest refrains from saying Whose name it is. V. 30: "raised" refers to the sending of Jesus to Israel (as in **3.**26); the resurrection is mentioned in the next verse. "A tree"=the cross of Calvary is meant, but the implication is clear. Jesus died under a curse (Deut. **21.**22,23; Gal. **3.**13) voluntarily assumed for the sake of sinners, as Peter was later to teach (1 Pet. **2.**24). V. 31: see on **3.**15. *Cf.* Luke **24.**47*f.* which includes the note of witness (in 32). The apostles were fulfilling their commission to the letter.

Acts 5.33-42

At Pentecost the reaction to Peter's Gospel call was penitent acceptance; here it is enraged hatred and refusal. The Gospel is ever a divider of men (see 2 Cor. **2.**14-16).

The intervention and speech of Gamaliel offers an interesting sidelight. Its first effect was to save the apostles from their fate (33). Gamaliel was a Pharisaic member of the Council, and greatly esteemed. He belonged to the liberal wing of his party, as a disciple of Rabbi Hillel; and was the teacher of Saul of Tarsus (**22.**3), who quite probably supplied Luke with the information here recorded.

His policy speech is typically Pharisaic in temper and content. It picks up the leading point in their theology—that God rules the world by a wise providence which is over all. "Everything is in the hand of heaven, except the fear of heaven," the Rabbis taught. That is, all is under divine control, but man is required to obey God and leave the issues with Him.

Two notable uprisings had already proved abortive, Gamaliel reminded them. Let the new movement work itself out; if it is not of God, it is bound to fail, as did the Messianic rebellions of Theudas and Judas the Galilean. If God is really in it, no human opposition can break it. Is this really a valid argument (*i*) to test early Christianity; (*ii*) to test later movements in the history of the Church?

Notes: V. 36: there was a rebel named Theudas whose disaffection against Rome was crushed in A.D. 44-46, according to Josephus. But this is an impossible identification, for at the time of Gamaliel's speech it had not happened. The name Theudas was common, and it is likely that an earlier (pre-A.D. 6, when Judas of Galilee was defeated, v. 37) uprising is referred to. V. 37: the census in this verse occurred in A.D.6-7, but is not the one mentioned in Luke **2.**2, which was before 4 B.C. V. 38: the counsel is "wait and see", but at least one of Gamaliel's students was not willing to accept this restraint. See **8.**3.

V. 41: "the name", almost a substitute word for their Christian principles and faith, as in 3 John 7.
To think over: (i) *"The same sun which softens wax hardens clay"*—is this an adequate explanation of the difference referred to in the first paragraph of this comment? (ii) How may we know where loyalty to civil and religious authority ceases in obedience to a higher allegiance? See Rom. **13.***1f.; 1 Pet.* **2.***12-17.*

Acts 6.1-7

Today's verses sketch the background to an important innovation in the early Church. Within the Jerusalem community where (*i*) a pooling of material resources was practised (**2.**44*f.*; **4.**34*f.*) and (*ii*) the influx of new converts was a notable feature (**5.**14; **6.**7), dissension arose over precisely these two developments, as v. 1 makes plain. The church, moreover, was divided on a cultural and linguistic basis, one side holding fast to its Palestinian tradition and speaking Aramaic, the other side being more open to the influences of Greek culture and using that language. Hence the two terms, "Hebrews" and "Hellenists". In later years this difference of emphasis hardened into clear opposition. The Hebrew Christians were fearful that a denial of the Law would lead to a relaxed morality; the more liberal Hellenistic Jewish believers saw the opportunities for missionary expansion, and under Stephen and Paul caught the vision of a worldwide Christian Church, reaching out to all nations.

The matter of the allotment of funds to necessitous widows was immediately attended to by the apostles. They gave the Hellenists a share in the administration, for, to judge from their names (5), all seven men belonged to that wing of the fellowship. They were commissioned with the full blessing of the Twelve (6).

A further note is added to call attention to the ongoing life of the Church, and its influence among even the priestly families in Jerusalem. There have been recent attempts to define more closely the identity of these priests (in the light of the Dead Sea scrolls and the Epistle to the Hebrews), but they are all speculative.

Notes: V. 2: the duties of the seven men are given as "serving tables". This is usually taken to mean some financial work in connection with the common fund. But it may be that they were to have responsibility for the *agape*-meal (see note on **2.**46) or love-feast, which also meant the task of sharing out the food to the poor (1). Of the seven in verse 5, two are more renowned for their preaching ministry. Which two? Notice the exemplary spiritual qualification needed. V. 5: all have

Greek-sounding names; one of them was not a born Jew, namely Nicolaus, a proselyte=a convert to Judaism. V. 6: the people chose and appointed the men, often called "deacons" (in view of the description in 1 Tim. 3.8-13); the apostles confirmed the choice by a solemn rite of ordination, after the Jewish pattern of "setting apart".

Acts 6.8—7.1

The most prominent member of the "seven" who were appointed to represent the Hellenists was Stephen. He is a key-figure in early Christian history, chiefly because of the powerful grasp that he had of the universal character of the Gospel which went beyond all national and racial boundaries. For that reason, his speech is reported in detail.

In these verses Stephen is introduced. His personal "charm" (8) and effective ministry (8) are mentioned. He stood in a true apostolic succession (*cf.* the wording here with 5.12). His opponents, drawn from a synagogue which called itself "a meeting-place for Freedmen" and who represented Hellenistic Jews from the world of the Dispersion, challenged him to debate. When they failed to answer him by fair means, they resorted to foul (11,12). The indictment was the same as that which was brought against Jesus: a remarkable fact, and one further proof of the continuity of the witness against Judaism, begun by the Lord and maintained by His servants who had grasped the inner meaning of His mission (Mark 2.21,22).

But false witnesses sometimes correctly hint at the truth. It is quite likely that he had spoken out against the sacrificial system, the venerable place of the Temple and the final authority of the Law—to judge from his later speech in chapter 7. He certainly made it clear that God's ultimate word was to be found in Jesus, not Moses (14). And that was a blasphemous remark in any Jew's ears (11).

Notes: V. 8: "grace" in Luke can often mean "graciousness" (Luke 4.22). V. 9: the place names indicate the original homes of men who had either received their civil freedom and citizenship or inherited it from their fathers. Saul of Tarsus is a notable instance of such a case (22.28), and it is tempting to find his presence in this dispute in view of the reference to Cilicia (see 21.39) and his later appearance at Stephen's martyrdom (7.58; 8.1). V. 10: *cf.* Luke 21.15. V. 11: Moses came to stand for all that was holiest and most valued in Rabbinic religion. Hence to deny him was to strike at the divine authority and validity of the entire Jewish system. This was a radical attack on

Judaism, which the earlier apostles had not made (*cf.* Peter's observance of the Temple worship). V. 14: Stephen had evidently perceived the inner significance of the Lord's promise (in John 2.19-21), and the thought of a new temple (Eph. 2.20*f.*; 1 Pet. 2.5). V. 15: his face, no less than Moses' (Ex. 34.29*f.*), shone with a heavenly glow.

Acts 7.2-29

What Stephen said to the Jewish council is sometimes called his defence (*i.e.*, an answer to the legal charges brought against him); but it is clearly more of an *apology*—that is, a statement of the teaching which had led to his arrest and prosecution. And as his doctrine touched the vital questions of Judaism's validity and his own "blasphemy" against God, his address turns out to be an *apologia pro vita sua*.

There are three chief ideas which his lengthy re-telling of the Old Testament story is designed to emphasize: (*i*) the Jewish people, throughout their long history, have been inveterately rebellious against God and His accredited messengers; (*ii*) God does not live in, nor does He desire, a material and fixed shrine. His presence is not confined to sacred sites, but accompanies His people, who are to be always a "pilgrim Church" on earth; and (*iii*) as a subsidiary theme, the Jewish people have not only rebelled against God and their leaders, they have consistently rejected the saviours whom God sent to them—the outstanding proof of this trait is to be seen in their recent rejection of their Messiah.

In Egypt Joseph was God's answer to the threat of patriarchal extinction; but he suffered much indignity at the hands of his brothers (9). Moses, too, in a later period appeared as a heaven-sent deliverer, but he met opposition and misunderstanding (23*ff.*).

So far Stephen has been patiently laying the foundations of his argument. Later, he will draw some unwelcome conclusions, as far as his hearers are involved.

Notes: V. 2: the call to Abraham, given in verse 3, is placed *before* his removal to Haran. Gen. 11.31*ff.* give it *after* his arrival there; but Gen. 15.7 shows that God was responsible for his leaving Ur, and this implies some communication with the patriarch. V. 4: see note in the I.V.F. *New Bible Commentary* on Gen. 11.26—12.5. V. 6: "aliens"— "a theme throughout the speech" (F. F. Bruce). *Cf.* Heb. 11.8-16. V. 14: the Hebrew text of Gen. 46.27; Ex. 1.5; Deut. 10.22 gives the number as seventy; but the Septuagint reads seventy-five. V. 20: an addition to the Old Testament account found in Philo. V. 22: again, extra-biblical sources (Josephus, Philo) comment on the wisdom and accomplishments of Moses in Egypt. Stephen shows acquaintance with these traditions.

Acts 7.30-53

Stephen's recital of Israel's history continues. The purpose of the long paragraph on Moses' call by God and his unique place as both deliverer (30-36) and lawgiver (37,38) is simply to show that Moses, of all Israel's national figures, enjoyed divine appointment and authority. But, in spite of these clear signs of attestation from God, he met with opposition and disbelief. Notice the asides which Stephen cleverly inserts: (25,35,39).

As a further indication of the failure of the Jewish nation, even when blessed with such an outstanding man of God as Moses, is given in the positive act of idolatry and apostasy which they committed (40,41,53). It was bad enough that they rebelled against Moses; it was far worse that they lapsed into flagrant idol worship and astrology (42).

At the same time as they practised a heathen worship, they imagined that God could be localized in a man-made shrine (built by Solomon, 47), and, further, they contrived to placate God by a multitude of sacrifices. Both these errors indicate bad religion, as the eighth-century prophets in Israel were quick to expose. But this prophetic protest went unheeded.

Stephen found the same hard core of resistance in his hearers; and his impassioned peroration (51-53) drove home the personal application in the light of the ample evidence. What precise points in his speech made them so angry (54)?

Notes: V. 34: with God's summons to send him to Pharaoh, Moses is thus uniquely qualified (35); and his later exploits demonstrated his authority from God (36). V. 37: see 3.22. V. 39: Stephen indicts the *motive* which inspired the worship of the golden calf. V. 42: *cf.* Rom. 1.24,26,28 for this fearful sentence. Vs. 42 and 43 are quoted from a Greek translation, of Amos 5.25*ff*. This explains the difference in wording from our English version. V. 44: God's intention is expressed in the making of a mobile tent (suitable for a pilgrim people); the permanent structure of Solomon's temple was a second-best, for reasons given in Isa. 66.1*f.* V. 51: as the unfaithful Jews did, according to Isa. 63.10. V. 52: *cf.* Matt. 23. 29-37. "The Righteous One" is a name for the Messiah (3.14).

Acts 7.54—8.1a

A colourless neutrality was impossible in view of the forthright declarations in Stephen's speech. The violent language of verse 54 makes it clear that he had touched his hearers on a tender spot; and they reacted by cutting short his sermon in an outburst of rage.

Note the one final "blasphemy"—from their point of view—which called forth the murderous spite of verses 57 and 58.

Stephen died, like his Master, with a prayer of committal and forgiveness on his lips (Luke 23.34,46). His death was probably more a lynching than a judicial execution for blasphemy; there was no trial, and Jewish law had an elaborate arrangement to safeguard the guilty person, accused of blasphemy and therefore condemned to death by stoning, if he should recant or if a witness for the defence should suddenly appear on the scene. Then the stoning must be stopped. It seems clear that no such precautions were made for Stephen's benefit; and he fell victim to the mob violence of an uncontrolled crowd. The most impressionable person in this sordid scene seems to have been Saul, who both looked after the witnesses' clothes—these witnesses for the prosecution were to carry out the sentence, according to Lev. 24.14; Deut. 17.7 (*cf.* John 8.7)—and, by his complicity, agreed with the rough "justice" meted out. He never forgot this awful sight (Acts 22.20), and his personal involvement in such violence (1 Tim. 1.13). Yet this martyrdom may have been the turning-point in his life, as Augustine believed: "If Stephen had not prayed, the Church would not have had Saul".

Notes: V. 55: Stephen's vision is full of meaning, and gives the key to his whole thought. He sees the exalted Jesus as victorious Son of Man, destined like the celestial Figure of Daniel 7.13*ff.* to possess world-dominion, and worthy of worship. Here is the clear statement of Stephen's Christology: he "saw that the Messiah was on the throne of the Universe" (W. Manson), and so by implication the Head of a worldwide Church. His characteristic name for Jesus is "Lord", which has the same implication, and he calls upon Him in prayer (so confessing His place within the God-head). Vs. 59, 60: the links with Luke's Passion story are important. He has captured the spirit of the dying Jesus, Who rises to greet the first Christian martyr. Contrast 2 Chron. 24.22.

Acts 8.1b-8

As a direct consequence of Stephen's speech and its sequel, an anti-

Christian outbreak scattered the Jerusalem Church. Why were the apostles exempt from this (1c)?

Some slight relief comes in the record of the kindly action of some Jews (or Jewish-Christians, 2) who buried Stephen, thus showing their abhorrence of this deed. By stark contrast, Saul felt no such regret—or, if he did, he silenced the voice of conscience by redoubling his efforts against the Church (3).

Vs. 4-8 take the reader into Samaria, the scene of Christian activity under the ministry of Philip, one of the "seven" (**6.5**). Again it is the Hellenistic-Christian representative who blazes a trail of evangelism outside Judea, and it is a further step in the onward and outward march of Christ's kingdom, according to the programme of **1.8**.

"A city of Samaria" was probably Gitta, where, according to an early Christian (Justin Martyr, who was a native of Samaria), Simon Magus (9) was born. Some features of evangelism in such a situation are recorded: the proclamation of the message which centred in the Messiah (5); the evidential accompaniment of signs (6,7) both in exorcism of foul spirits and in bodily healings—note that these two aspects seem to be distinguished; and an upsurge of spiritual "joy", as a direct gift of the Holy Spirit according to Rom. **14.17**; **15.13**; Gal. **5.22**. *Consider how far these features are to be expected today in the Church's evangelistic work? Are they in fact found in your church?*

Notes: V. 1: persecution leads to further expansion on the principle that (*i*) "the blood of the martyrs is seed" (Tertullian); and (*ii*) dispersed Christians share their faith over a wider area. The Greek verb in v. 4 is the farmer's word for sowing seed across a field. Collect some of the N.T. passages on the theme of sowing and reaping, like Mark **4**; 2 Cor. **9**.6-15; Gal. **6**.7-10; 2 Tim. **2.6**. V. 2: "devout men" is a term usually associated with Jews (as **2.5**; Luke **2.25**), but occasionally it is used of Jewish-Christians (**22.12**). V. 3: "laid waste", lit. "ravage"—or even "savage"—the lexicon gives it in regard to a wild beast's tearing at a carcase. There are four references in the epistles to Saul's persecuting zeal. Can you discover them? One is given in yesterday's portion.

Acts 8.9-24

Vs. 9-13 concentrate on one special case among the multitudes (6) who showed interest in Philip's preaching and healing. Simon had already acquired a reputation before Philip appeared (10,11), and quite likely saw his popularity about to wane and his livelihood to be in danger by his competitor's success. He therefore suggested an alliance, and feigned belief (12,13; but v. 21 is clear on his motive) even to the extent of openly identifying himself with the Christian cause.

Vs. 14-24 show how Simon fared when the apostles came to visit Samaria. Note the purpose of their coming. And what followed in regard to those Samaritans who had professed faith in Christ. Were they believers *before* Peter and John laid hands on them?

The clash between Peter and Simon well illustrates the spiritual gift of percipience which the apostle had (see 5.3,4). Simon betrays his secret motive in a request for the Holy Spirit's power as though it were like a piece of magic (19). He wanted the power to enhance his own reputation as a wonder-worker. Peter tartly refuses, and speaks right to the point (20-23). Verse 23 means in modern language: "I see you are still an unconverted reprobate" (J. A. Findlay)—so much for his earlier profession of belief and his acceptance of baptism! Simon's reaction is vague (24), but probably it means a weak plea to escape punishment, like King Saul's (1 Sam. 24.16; 26.21).

Notes: V. 9: Simon the magician plays an important role in early Christian literature as the father of heresy. V. 10: means that he regarded himself as the unique agent of "the supreme God" (probably a syncretistic name for God in some Oriental-Greek religions). V. 13: was he sincere, or (as suggested above) a charlatan? Lucian was later to write about such bogus "believers" who traded upon simple Christians and made an easy living that way. V. 14: John had been to Samaria before (*cf.* Luke 9.54). V. 15: for other sequences of believing, baptizing and receiving the Spirit, see Acts 10.44*ff.*; 19.5*f.*; Eph. 1.13. V.16: "it"—R.S.V. needs correction here. The Holy Spirit is a Person. V. 17: this has been called a Samaritan "Pentecost" (by G. W. H. Lampe), and apostolic authorization is thus given to a new phase of the Church's outreach as "a new nucleus of the missionary Church has been established" (Lampe).

Questions: Did Simon receive the laying on of hands (17, 18)—or was his "wickedness" (22) detected before that? What is today's counterpart to Peter's gift of discernment (1 John 4.1-6)?

Acts 8.25-40

The Church's leaders leave Samaria (25) once their mission is achieved. Philip, however, received a direct summons to keep a lonely rendezvous on the Gaza road (26). The other party in the interview was a well-connected courtier, an official in the service of the Candace (a hereditary title borne by Ethiopean queens; "Ethiopia"=Nubia). At Jerusalem where, probably as a "God-fearer" (see comment on **10.**2*f.*), he had worshipped Israel's God, he had also acquired a scroll of the book of Isaiah in Greek. The ensuing conversation proceeds by the method of question and answer. Note the three queries which the Ethiopian expresses (31,34,36). The evangelist's answers are straightforward and of immediate help (a lesson here for all Christian counsellors today). Philip becomes the interpreter of Scripture, the evangelist with a single text (35), and the baptizer of a new convert (38).

The Spirit of God Who first directed Philip's footsteps (26: here called "an angel of the Lord") and gave him accurate guidance to the place of human need (29) now separates the two men (39). Why?

Notes: V. 26: "desert" may refer to Gaza, in which case the road ran from Jerusalem to Old Gaza, destroyed by Alexander the Great in 332 B.C. and in ruins at that time. V. 27: Ethiopia is not the modern Abyssinia, but North Sudan. Vs. 32, 33: a citation from the Suffering Servant poems in Isaiah, interpreted by Philip as fulfilled in Jesus' life and death, following the example of Jesus' own application of these passages to His ministry (*e.g.*, Mark **10.**45). V.35: "opened his mouth" —rabbinical idiom for a lecture on Scripture. V. 36: some instruction on faith and baptism is clearly implied, leading to the eunuch's request. V. 37 is relegated to the R.S.V. margin as an addition of the Western text. It represents, however, an early baptismal procedure of interrogation and response of faith. Notice the "creed" which the eunuch confessed. V. 39: the same Western text adds a reference to the Holy Spirit's coming on the new believer. V. 40: in a walking trance, Philip came to himself at Azotus—was it a spiritual elation which upheld him?

Meditation: Consider Philip as "the evangelist" (**21.**8).

Acts 9.1-9

Saul of Tarsus, briefly introduced at **8.**1, now re-appears in what is a turning-point in the narrative of Acts. Indeed, what this section describes is the turning-point in the life of this man, destined to become the dominant character in the remainder of Luke's history as the divinely-chosen apostle to the Gentiles (Gal. **1.**16). The Lord's intention in **9.**15 is the key to what is written in today's portion. And it is indisputable that "What happened on the Damascus road is the most important event in the history of Christianity from Pentecost to our own day" (F. F. Bruce).

The right of extradition was given to the high priest by the Roman authorities; and Saul had already shown promise as an able persecutor of the Christians (**8.3**).

The encounter with the living Christ is told with a simplicity and naturalness of any reported conversation (4-6); but the circumstances of both the vision and the voice are altogether remarkable. Which Old Testament prophet(s) received a heavenly summons by what they saw of God's glory and what they heard from the heavenly throne?

The "light from heaven" (3) outshone the noon sun (**22.**6; **26.**13) and is a frequent Old Testament symbol of the divine presence. The voice (4) has a counterpart in the Rabbinic *bath qol* (lit., the daughter of a voice) by which when God speaks in heaven an echo of His voice is heard on earth. The supernaturalness of what Saul saw and heard is clear. His companions were arrested (7), but only Saul was able to understand the *meaning* of what the voice said (v. 7 is expanded in **22.**9) and Whom the vision represented. Moreover, only he was affected by the excess of light (**22.**11).

Not much was revealed at that time to the future apostle (6); but he was "a new man in Christ" (2 Cor. **5.**17) from that moment. In that brief encounter his past life flashed before him—a thought he could never efface (1 Tim. **1.**12-14); and his terrible crime of wounding the Christ in His people appeared in a heinous light—which again he always remembered (1 Cor. **8.**12). Above all, this was his moment with the living Lord who called him by name (John **10.**3,14) and was answered "Lord, what wilt Thou have me to do?" (Verse 6 in A.V. which translates an inferior text, but the thought is found in **22.**10).

Acts 9.10-19

Everything we learn about Ananias, the Jewish-Christian disciple (**22.**12), is commendable and edifying. He is human enough to express incredulity that such a notorious arch-enemy as Saul should have been converted (13,14), but believing enough to go without hesitation and fear (17) upon the Lord's errand, and charitable enough to greet his former persecutor as "Brother Saul", a word which would have stuck in the throat of any lesser man than Ananias. Ananias goes down in history as the first Christian influence on a newly-awakened Saul, by what he said (17) and what he did (12,18; **22.**14-16)—the first in a line of men and women to whom Paul later paid tribute as his predecessors in the faith (Rom. **16.**7). The formative influences we receive in the first days of our Christian life greatly influence our subsequent future. Hence the exacting role of Ananias which he performed admirably. Two visions, one conveying instructions to Ananias of what he was to do, and the other making known to the blinded Saul the person he was to expect, brought the two men together. Moreover, Saul would be recognized by what he was doing in Judas' house. Note what it was (11).

Saul's future destiny is carefully described in v. 15, which strikes the notes which the later record will amplify: he will fulfil a ministry, like that of Isaiah's elect Servant, and bring the news of salvation to the Gentiles (**13.**47, quoting Isa. **49.**6), but the price to be paid will be costly (16). Col. **1.**24 and his ultimate martyrdom (2 Tim. **4.**6 looks forward to this) tell us something of that cost.

Notes: V. 12: the "laying on of hands" was a Jewish rite with many meanings. Here the sense is one of solemn ordination or setting apart for God's service (as Jewish rabbis were ordained). The gift of the Holy Spirit (17) is associated with this commissioning, but the Head of the Church alone can impart this, as **26.**16 and Eph. **4.**7 make clear. In any case Ananias was no priest! He seems to have administered the baptism (**22.**16).

Acts 9.19-25

Vs. 19b-25 show how seriously Paul took his new vocation as a man "saved to serve". Mark the word "immediately" (20). Where does the record of Gal. **1.**15*ff.* fit in to this period? The answer is supplied in 2 Cor. **11.**32. See below.

The preaching of the Christian apostle is set in the synagogue, which may be a little surprising. Yet Saul was a Jewish rabbi, albeit now converted to the Messiah, and entitled to address the assembled congregation at their worship. Saul's first opportunities came in this way, during his first missionary tour (**13.**14*ff.*). The rift came at **18.**4-7. Some idea of what Saul said in these messages is given in verses 20, 22: Jesus as Son of God (in the sense of Psalm **2.**7; the enthroned Messianic King, and Rom. **1.**3,4: a pre-Pauline confessional formula) and the true Messiah of Israel Who fulfilled the prophecies.

Vs. 23-25 describe the first of the many hazards to which his life was exposed. Perhaps we should insert before these verses a departure for "Arabia", inhabited by the Nabatean Arabs. Their leader was Aretas, who heard something of his ministry in his kingdom as Saul preached to the Nabateans (Gal. **1.**17). When he returned to Damascus, Aretas' ethnarch was instructed to seize him with the help of evilly-disposed Jews in the city (23). But Saul too had his helpers, called "his disciples", since his powers of leadership were already being felt, who assisted his escape through a hole in the city wall (2 Cor. **11.**33).

Notes: V. 21: titles for early Christian believers are interesting. Those "who called on this Name" (*cf.* 14) means men and women devoted to the worship and service of Jesus as their God. The exact expression comes from the Old Testament—*e.g.*, Genesis **21.**33—and lasted on into the Pauline church vocabulary (1 Cor. **1.**2). The title "saints" (**9.**13), meaning "dedicated to God's service", is mainly employed in describing the Jerusalem community (Rom. **15.**26).

To ponder: "Are you a converted Jew?" a Hebrew-Christian was once asked. "No," he replied, "I am a completed Jew." So Saul preached.

Acts 9.26-31

Vs. 26-30. This short paragraph is full of men and movement. Saul, the Jerusalem disciples and their leaders, the apostles, Barnabas and Hellenistic Jews are mentioned; and from the parallel account in Galatians **1.**18-24 we can identify the apostles as Peter, and James the Lord's brother.

Saul removes from Damascus to Jerusalem (26) where he meets a natural suspicion on the part of those who only recently had cause to fear his bitter persecution (**8.**3; **9.**21). How could they trust his motives? He finds an advocate in Barnabas (27), who disarms all criticism on the score that (*i*) Saul had met the risen Lord Who spoke to him—observe the naturalness of this conversion-description; and (*ii*) he had "won his spurs" in his bold witnessing for Christ at Damascus. Saul could never turn back now.

His further movements at Jerusalem are recorded. "The words 'coming in and going out' at Jerusalem do not mean that he visited places outside the city, but that he moved about freely and fearlessly in and out of houses in the city" (McNeile-Williams); and continued an intrepid ministry of forthright proclamation. His approach to the Greek-speaking Jews, however, met with some opposition. Like Stephen before him, he found himself embroiled in religious controversy (the bitterest sort of controversy!) (V. 29: "disputed" is the same verb as in **6.**9). Not for the first time (**9.**23), his life was threatened. Again, Christian friends came to his aid, and conducted him to

Caesarea, the Mediterranean sea-town. Thence he sailed to his home city of Tarsus in Cilicia (Gal. 1.21). I wonder what his family and their friends would have made of him at this time, as he did according to Mark 5.19.

V. 31. Paul leaves the stage at this point, later to re-enter at 11.25. Peter comes back into the chief role; and the transition is marked by this summary of the (Palestinian) Church's progress and expanding influence.

Notes: V. 27: the plural "apostles" is not in conflict with the two names of Galatians 1.18*f.*; and "the churches of Judaea which were in Christ" describe (as in 1 Thess. 2.14) Jewish-Christians *outside* the holy city to which at that time Saul was personally unknown. V. 29: Hellenists are Jews of the Greek-speaking world (R.V., Grecian Jews), like Saul himself. (See Acts 6.1 and comment.)

Acts 9.32-43

Saul's conversion and its aftermath has been a significant interlude to Luke's history. Now the historian returns to one of his central themes, namely, to chronicle the progress of the Gospel as it embraced the non-Jewish world. Peter's adventures, continued in chapters 10, 11 and 12, point forward to the subsequent Gentile mission. Indeed, the rather vague phrase "Peter went here and there among them all" (32) may look back to 8.25, where Peter and his companions are last mentioned.

Bedridden Aeneas may have belonged to the Christian group at Lydda, perhaps formed following the evangelistic work of Philip in 8.40 in those parts. In words which are reminiscent of the healing stories in the gospels (*e.g.*, Mark 2.11) Peter bids the paralyzed man get up and "get yourself something to eat" (34; this translation, preferred by some translators, then re-echoes Mark 5.43). Can we see here an attention to a patient's needs agreeable to the professional interest of Luke "the dear doctor" (Col. 4.14)?

Vs. 36-43. Joppa was originally a Philistine city, and populated in New Testament times by Greeks. Peter's message and ministry are reaching out with a remarkable breadth of sympathy and concern; and we may ponder the fact that he is willing to lodge with Simon, a tanner—*i.e.*, one engaged in a ceremonially unclean and defiling occupation from the Jewish point of view.

Tabitha's name is similar to the call "talitha" (in Mark 5.41) as two forms of the same name, meaning "my gazelle"; but this coincidence is not significant, even though the Lord's raising of Jairus' daughter and Peter's ministrations follow a similar pattern. What points of correspondence can you spot? The disciple has caught his Master's spirit.

Notes: V. 37: washing was a Jewish practice as a rite of purification. V. 39: a touching scene, especially if we give full value to the verb's true meaning: they showed *on themselves* the coats and garments which Dorcas had made—a Petrine memory, passed on to Luke. V. 41: Peter's helping hand is again outstretched (3.7).

Acts 10.1-8

Cornelius's status is referred to in a few verses in this chapter—verses 2, 4, 22 and 35. What sort of picture can you build up of this man's character from these descriptions?

From a professional standpoint he was a Roman centurion and a Gentile (1), but a Gentile who was attracted to the Jewish faith and way of life, although not a fully committed proselyte. Persuaded by Jewish monotheism (belief in one, righteous God) and morality, he is known by the technical term of "God-fearer" (2), and this for him was no empty profession, as an angel, and his servants, and Peter, all confirm. What an excellent set of character references he had!

Cornelius is chosen for the signal honour of receiving the Gospel and its benefits at the hands of Peter as the latter exercises the "power of the keys". See Matthew **16.**19. He is the first-fruits of the great Roman world to be led to faith in Christ under the apostolic ministry; and his conversion is a notable watershed in the book of Acts, as **11.**17, 18 recognize.

Notes: V. 1: "Italian Cohort"—a company of six hundred men. There is evidence that *Cohors II Italica* was stationed in Syria in A.D. 60-70, and Caesarea was the military headquarters of Roman government in Palestine. V. 2: these are the marks of Jewish piety, characteristic of a "God-fearer" (see too in **13.**16, 26; **16.**14; **18.**7). V. 3: at 3 p.m. the vision came, but probably it was too late for the men to set off for Joppa, some thirty miles away, that day. So they left on the next day (9) and arrived at noon. V. 4: almsgiving is likened to a Levitical sacrifice (Lev. **2.**2, 9, 16; *cf.* Psa. **141.**2: Heb. **13.**15*f.*; Phil. **4.**18). V. 6: Simon lived by the seaside where (*i*) he used sea-water for his trade, and (*ii*) caused no ceremonial (nor social!) offence to the Jews who abhorred that odorous trade.

Question: *But His angels here are human,*
(Not) the shining hosts above.

Which line fits the visitor of verse 3? Verse 20 suggests the second, but verse 30 could be taken in the sense of "angel" = messenger = human agent, sent by God.

Acts 10.9-16

Cornelius' vision at Caesarea has its counterpart in Peter's vision at Joppa to which the messengers have been sent. While they are making the thirty-mile journey Peter is made ready to receive the request they bring by a special revelation in the form of a symbolic vision.

The noon hour (9) probably indicates the second period of prayer in the Jewish habit of prayer three times daily (see Psa. 55.17; Dan. 6.10). The heavenly vision consisted of a large object resembling a sheet (a ship's sail?) let down from above and holding a menagerie of the animal kingdom. The point to notice is that clean and unclean animals, according to the levitical rule (Lev. 11), jostled together indiscriminately; and the divine command of verse 13 makes no discrimination. This accounts for Peter's horrified disavowal (14) and the answer to his objection (15: which verse in the Gospel of Mark does this call to mind? Perhaps Peter is responsible for the editorial note which is what Mark 7.19b really is, as R.S.V. makes clear). Lest he should mistake the meaning or imagine that he was dreaming, the vision is renewed three times (16).

But what is the meaning? Clearly it has to do with the cancellation of the Jewish food-laws which allow some diets and forbid certain others. That in itself was revolutionary enough, as the debate between the Lord and the Pharisees (in Mark 7.1-23) illustrates. But there is a deeper sense which Peter was later to grasp more fully. As a Jew he would at the time of the vision regard the Gentile people as religiously "defiled" (the description in Galatians 2.15 is an apt summary of Jewish mentality and exclusiveness) and so beyond the reach of friendship. And to have a meal with a Gentile would be unthinkable, for meal-time was a solemn and sacred occasion, begun in a prayer of blessing over food and continued by religious conversation. The abolishing of the ancient dietary laws is a token from God that there is no barrier to keep the Jews and Gentiles apart any longer. As Paul put it, the middle wall of partition has been broken down in Christ (Eph. 2.11-18).

Notes: V. 10: literally, "he experienced an ecstasy". V. 11: "four corners", obviously metaphorical. V. 12: see Gen. **6**.20. V. 14: it is a foolhardy man who contradicts the Lord. *Do we ever try?*

Acts 10.17-33

Notice that the angelic visitor's message is attributed to the Holy Spirit (19-20) Who spoke to His servant both in the trance-vision (10*ff.*) and through the inward monition of his own reflection (17, "inward perplexity" required Peter to "ponder the vision", 19).

Peter's hospitality—an important virtue in early Christianity—delayed the departure until the following day (23a).

Vs. 23b-29. The time-notices are not easy to follow; and it is possible that "the next day" of verse 23 is the same as "the following day" of verse 24, if the journey of thirty miles took the same time as that of the early messengers. The Western text in verse 30 reads, "It is *three* days ago". Otherwise, if we read "four days ago", the reckoning is inclusive or the return trip for the messengers took longer.

In this way Peter the Christian apostle and Cornelius the Gentile enquirer were brought together. Why did the latter prostrate himself and do homage (25)? What steps had he taken to ensure a good reception of the message from God which Peter was to bring (24,27, 33)? The courtesy and modesty of verse 33 should be particularly noted. (Are these excellent qualities found in us in our correspondence and conversation with other believers?) "Did ever a preacher of the Gospel have a more promising audience than this?" (F. F. Bruce).

Notes: V. 20: the key phrase is "without hesitation" (*cf.* similar words in v. 29). This is explained by v. 28. Peter as a Jew might well hesitate before accepting the invitation to visit a Gentile, and object to eating under his roof. Such an act would lead to a ceremonial defilement. But the vision of verses 9-16 had changed all this. V. 25: *cf.* Rev. **19**.10; **22**.8,9. V. 28: Jewish rules virtually forbade loyal Jews from accepting Gentile hospitality, chiefly because of the fear that the food provided might not be *kosher* (*i.e.*, ritually slaughtered, with the blood drained away) and perhaps harmful, if it had previously been used in idol-worship. 1 Cor. **8** may be compared.

Question: The whole question of God's revelation to man is involved here. How does God speak to us today?

Acts 10.34-48

This memorable sermon is important for a variety of good reasons: (*i*) it represents the *first* offer of the Gospel to the Gentile world, and so paves the way for a full-scale Gentile mission; (*ii*) it gives an outline of what the early Christians believed about the significance of Jesus' ministry, death, and triumph. Not by accident, therefore, it contains a ground-plan (in 37-40) of the later Gospel of St. Mark, which Christian tradition has associated with Peter's preaching. "Peter related, Mark wrote" (Jerome); (*iii*) addressed to a Gentile congregation (35), it received the approbation of God in a way which few sermons do. The preacher's voice was silenced by a gracious interposition (44) and a remarkable outpouring of the Holy Spirit (45). The main point to grasp lies in the phrase "even on the Gentiles". In an apt phrase, this has been called the Gentile Pentecost, and shows the fulfilment of what Peter had hinted at in 2.39. Work out the steps by which God prepared the Church for this decisive turning-point.

The structure of the sermon is worthy of close study. Peter begins by declaring that recent events have shown that there is no "most favoured nation" clause in God's covenant with His people. The Old Testament prophets had taught the same, with a doctrine of the remnant (the faithful Israelites within the larger group of the nation) and a universalistic outlook which comprehended the Gentiles within the scope of God's mercy and care. (There is no conflict between Israel's election and God's mercy to the nations; precisely *through* His elect people His love was intended to reach out to the Gentiles. Israel was elect for the sake of mankind.)

The terminal points of Jesus' ministry are John's baptism (37) and the witnesses to the empty tomb (41). He was the Messiah (38), marked out as God's saving Agent in His life, death, and vindication by God. The apostles are the accredited witnesses to all this (39,41), and the commissioned representatives of the Gospel message (42) whose offer fulfils the promise of the Old Testament (43). Turn up *one* Old Testament promise of forgiveness, now made good in the Gospel.

The effect of the preacher's words is notable. Peter compares it to his own experience on the day of Pentecost (47; *cf*. **11**.15-17). These Gentiles gave evidence by the use of "tongues" (46), and received Christian baptism (not administered by Peter, however, 48) as initiation into the visible fellowship of the Church. No mention of circumcision is made.

To think over: Go through Peter's sermon again and compare it with what the Apostles' Creed says of our Lord Jesus Christ.

Acts 11.1-18

The good work of Peter's ministry now comes under fire! Note who its critics are (2). And what charge they bring against him (3).

The apostle's defence occupies the next section, and goes over the same ground as in ch. **10**. Why has Luke taken obvious pains to repeat the details of this incident? Certainly this account, in Peter's own words, has a vividness and colour all its own. Pick out some of the interesting additions and personal turns of phrase which Peter's own account gives: for example, "it came down to me" (5); "looking at it closely" (6); and verse 14. From verse 15a it seems that Peter was only getting started with his sermon when God's intervention took him and his congregation by surprise! Verse 17 implies that the Twelve became full believers and Christians only at Pentecost—*i.e.*, when they grasped the saving significance of the Cross and the risen Lord. The defence concludes on a note which could hardly be controverted. God Himself had borne witness to the rightness of His servant's action (17), and any refusal to accept the response as genuine and in line with His will would be tantamount to opposing Him.

In the face of such irrefutable logic, the Jewish-Christians accepted the conclusion of verse 18. Probably they did this with sincerity, but a more serious and sustained criticism was bound to arise once the evangelization of the Gentiles and their acceptance as church members without circumcision was made the rule rather than the exception. The Judaizers here were prepared to receive Cornelius and his group as an exceptional and isolated case; they were utterly opposed—as later history records—to the Pauline principle of a Church in which *all* distinctions of race were abolished (Gal. 3.27-29). What is the bearing of all this on the civil rights/colour question in the modern world?

Notes: V. 2: the tenets of this party are given in **15.**1. Hence their name. But at this stage their accusation is that Peter broke the ritual rules and ate with Gentiles. The issue over circumcision came later, and was raised as a bulwark against the prospect of a predominantly Gentile Church once the mission to the Gentiles got under way (**11.** 20,21) so auspiciously. V. 6: adds a fourth group to the list of **10.**12. V. 18: an admission that Peter was right—for the moment.

Acts 11.19-30

This is a short section, but packed with dynamite. It carries forward to the next crucial stage the widening expansion of the Church's outreach. At Antioch an unprecedented step was taken (20). Members of Stephen's school, who had caught and preserved his spirit and who represented the wide sympathies of Hellenistic Judaism, began an evangelistic approach to rank outsiders. Cornelius had been a Godfearer (*i.e.*, interested in the Jewish faith) before his conversion; the Greeks whom these men appealed to were completely untouched by Jewish influences. Yet they made a dramatic response to the proclamation of Jesus as Lord (21). Consider the significance of this title at this juncture (*cf.* 1 Cor. **12.2**,3).

The Jerusalem headquarters wanted to keep this movement under surveillance; and Barnabas was sent to Antioch, a city destined to become the springboard for the full-dress mission to the Gentile world (**13.1**).

It is not surprising that this city played such an important role in early Christianity. Situated near the coast of Syria, it was the capital of the Roman province. Its earlier history was shaped by Greek influences, yet it had received a great influx of Jewish population during the centuries of its life. It was thus the cosmopolitan centre of the Syrian world, a meeting-place of east and west. Greek culture and Jewish faith met and intermingled in a busy commercial emporium, and provided just the right conditions for the rise and growth of a Hellenistic Christian Church (24b).

Vs. 27-30 provide an interlude, chiefly to explain how it was that the churches came to contribute to the relief of the poverty-afflicted mother church in Jerusalem. The famine in Judea is dated by Josephus between A.D.44-48. The missionary apostles of Antioch are delegated to bring the gift to Jerusalem (30)—a visit probably to be equated with that of Galatians **2.1***ff.* if the letter to the Galatians is the first of the Pauline letters to be written.

Notes: V. 19 picks up the reference in **8.4**. The mention of Stephen's name is important in showing a continuance of his posthumous influence. V. 20: "preaching Jesus as Lord" (so Rom. **10.**9). V. 21: "turned to the Lord"—a characteristic description of Gentile conversions (**15.**19; Gal. **4.**9; 1 Thess. **1.**9). V. 23: the Gospel's effect upon human lives was *visible*! V. 26: first mention of "Christians"="partisans of Christ", as pagans viewed them (**26.**28; 1 Pet. **4.**16).

Acts 12.1-11

The next incident of the onward sweep of the Gospel which the reader expects is the kind of episode which chapter **13** narrates—namely, the first missionary journey of St. Paul. But one indication that the events of **11.**22-30 occupied a longer time than the text at first suggests may be that Luke places next a full account of Peter's adventures. At all events, our attention is switched from Paul to Peter.

"Herod the king" (1) is Herod Agrippa I, who found a friend in the Roman emperor Caligula who gave him the control of territory which belonged to the former's uncle Philip (Luke **3.**1), adding to it the district of Abilene governed by Lysanias. In A.D.37 Herod received the kingdom, and thereafter acquired the domain of Herod Antipas, the territories of Galilee and Perea. In A.D.41 he received the control of Judea; and this is the period indicated by the chronological note of verse 1: "about that time".

Two Christian leaders fell foul of Herod's violent pogrom. James was killed (fulfilling Mark **10.**39), Peter was arrested with a view to a later execution after the seven-day period of the Passover festival (3). Herod's malevolent design is darkly hinted in verses 4 and 6, where "to bring him out" implies an intended execution.

Peter's case seemed to be hopeless (notice the emphasis on "prison", "soldiers", "chains", "sentries" guarding the door in verses 4-6). But the Christians' secret weapon was being silently and secretly forged. What was it (5)?

Deliverance came in the form of a supernaturally-timed visitor's arrival (7). No barred doors prevented his entry; no guard impeded him and the bewildered Peter as they threaded their way through the gaol (10); no key was needed to open the last gate to freedom (10b).

Notes: V. 3: Passover lasted from Nisan 14 to Nisan 21 (Ex. **12.**18). Luke uses the term Passover (4) for the entire festival season, as in his gospel (**22.**1,7). V. 5: "earnest prayer"—this description is found in Luke **22.**44, *lit.*, "in a stretched-out manner". Prayer meant hard work for these devoted believers (Col. **4.**12). V. 7: "angel" and "messenger" are the same Greek term. Whichever translation is preferred, the deliverance was miraculous at every point.

Acts 12.12-17

The bewilderment of Peter was quickly dispelled as he came to himself (11) and took stock of his position (12: the same verb for his awareness is used again at **14.**6). The address he sought out is evidently (as a fourth-century tradition confirms) the place where the Last

Supper was held and the gift of the Spirit was awaited (**1.13,14**); and this was the scene of the church at prayer (**5**).

Some life-like touches make this one of the most gripping narratives in the New Testament. Each subsequent action is true to experience; the recognition of his Galilean accent; the disbelief with which her announcement was greeted; the attempt at rationalization ("it can't be Peter himself; it must be his guardian angel, impersonating his voice", **15**); and at length, as he kept on knocking, the decision to find out who it was by the simplest method—to open the gate! Then Peter came in, and with a characteristic gesture of the hand damped down the hubbub of excitement. ("If only you'll be quiet, I'll explain and tell you all about it".) What followed was a thrilling testimony to the Lord's grace and power—and an indirect rebuke to those who had met for specific prayer (**5**) and who wouldn't believe that the answer they sought was to be found outside the door, waiting to come in. The epistle of James has something to say on this topic (**1.6-8**).

Peter then departed for "another place", but no one knows exactly where. He is back in Jerusalem at chapter **15**, but at that time James, the Lord's brother, holds a commanding position in the church there. Perhaps he had filled the gap of leadership when Peter was in prison. Hence verse 17b.

Notes: V. 12: John Mark is the author of the gospel which bears his name and is the man of Col. **4.10**; Philem. 24; 2 Tim. **4.11**; 1 Pet. **5.13** as well as Acts **13.5**. V. 15: the idea of a guardian angel is found in Matt. **18.10**; Heb. **1.14**, and goes back to Gen. **48.16**. V. 17: no mention of the other apostles. They had left Jerusalem, as is possibly implied in **11.30**.

Questions: (*i*) *What problems of providence does this chapter raise? James is killed, but Peter survives by a miracle. Can we say why? Should we try?* (*ii*) *What lessons in prayer may we learn from this story?*

Acts 12.18-25

Not unnaturally there was an immediate sequel to the news of Peter's escape from prison. His guards suffered as a result of Herod's displeasure (**19**). But Herod himself was soon to meet a fateful end; verses 20-23 are a piece of secular history which is also recorded by Josephus in *Antiquities*, Book 19. Both accounts agree that he suffered a divine sentence of judgment on the score of his pride. In fact, both records are complementary, and throw light on each other.

It appears that the "appointed day" in Caesarea on which the people of Tyre and Sidon were to make a representation to the king

(20,21) was a festival in honour of the emperor, possibly the emperor's birthday (August 1). Both historians describe how Herod was greeted as a god (22), and Josephus adds: "He did not rebuke them, nor did he repudiate their impious flattery". His story goes on: he saw an owl, which he recognized as a messenger of evil tidings, and a pang of grief pierced his heart. Luke attributes this to a divine action (23), and his terrifying phrase, "he was eaten by worms and died", corresponds to the description which Josephus gives of violent abdominal pains which led to his eventual death five days later. The date is about A.D.44.

By vivid contrast "the word of God grew and multiplied" (24)—a reminder that earthly tyrants come and go, but even their cruel animosity is powerless to arrest the onward progress of the cause of God and His Church. In the bitter days of Julian the apostate, a scoffer asked a Christian, "What is your Carpenter doing now?" His quiet reply was: "Making a coffin for your emperor".

V. 25 poses a difficulty; the R.S.V. and R.S.V. margin giving two different versions of the direction in which Barnabas and Saul moved. As the story left them last at Jerusalem (11.30), the R.S.V. reads more naturally, but it translates a corrected text. As a third possibility the phrase "at Jerusalem" might be taken with what follows rather than with what precedes. Translate, then: "Barnabas and Saul returned (to Antioch), having completed their task in Jerusalem".
Meditation: Philippians 1.28,29.

Acts 13.1-12

The N.E.B. heads this chapter and new section: *The Church Breaks Barriers*. This is an accurate summary of the new phase of missionary activity begun by the Church at Antioch.

Vs. 1-3 describe how the new impetus was given. Note what the Church's preoccupation was when the Spirit's summons came (2) and why these two men were chosen. How were they commissioned (3)?

The first missionary tour is then detailed. From Seleucia, the port of Antioch, they came to Salamis, the chief town of Cyprus. Christian witness was made in the Jewish synagogues, mainly (so we may judge from verse 15) by seizing the opportunity which came to give a sermon to the assembled congregation in each place. *Cf.* Luke 4.15-30. John (Mark's) assistance suggests that he was a catechetical teacher, engaged in follow-up work (5).

The encounter with Elymas at Paphos is a reminder that the Gospel of Christ had many rivals in the ancient religious world. The lure of magic—which included such things as astrology, fortune-telling, healing and exorcism—was very powerful, and magicians practised their art all over the Roman world. Magical ideas invaded Judaism, chiefly from Chaldean sources; and Elymas was known also by a Jewish name (6).

Sergius Paulus, the Roman proconsul, shows a remarkable openness to the Christian message (7). This obviously displeased the magician, who had the wit to see that if his master became a believer in God his services would quickly be dispensed with. Hence his obstruction (8) which, in turn, met with a forthright statement from Paul (his Roman name is now used, as he comes to the fore, *cf.* verse 13, and takes precedence over Barnabas).

Notes: V. 1: these names are full of interest and embrace diverse racial and social groups. "Niger" means "darkie", and Symeon is possibly to be equated with Simon of Cyrene (Luke **23.**26). Lucius is not to be equated, however, with the evangelist Luke, nor with the Lucius of Romans **16.**21. Manaen had been well placed in Herod's entourage as the prince's "companion". V. 2: a precious sidelight on early Christian worship, which included a worshipping of Jesus as Lord. V. 5: R.S.V. disguises the presence of a technical expression here: John was their attendant (same word in Luke **1.**2). V. 12: no immediate conversion is explicit, but Ramsay has shown that there is inscriptional evidence of his family's becoming Christian in later times.

Acts 13.13-41

From this point in the book of Acts the name of "Paul" replaces the birth name "Saul" (*cf.* **13.**9) except in those few passages which tell again the story of his conversion (*e.g.*, **22.**7). The reason for this is that missionary activity moved on to Gentile territory where the apostle's Roman *cognomen* was more suitable. Moreover, for the first time, we read of "Paul and his company" (13). Barnabas has slipped into second place (contrast **12.**25; **13.**2 and **13.**43). Was this prominence now given to Paul the cause of Mark's defection (13b), as he saw his cousin (Col. **4.**10) passed over? More probably, it was that Mark never envisaged such an extensive penetration of Gentile country, as Paul and the party pressed on into Asia Minor.

The first goal of Paul's journey beyond the Taurus mountains was Antioch in Pisidia (14). Paul selects a place of strategic importance as a centre and base of apostolic ministry—Pisidian Antioch was a Roman colony. He makes full use of the synagogue as a sounding-board from which his message may go out.

Jewish worship gave opportunity for any qualified visitor to expound the Scriptures in the form of a "homily". Hence the invitation of verse 15. The apostle's sermon is an appeal to God's revelation under the old covenant. "The law and the prophets" (15; Rom. **3**.21) were his source of authority—at least as a preparation for, and witness to, the coming Christ of God. In this sermon his chief point rests with David (22), who prefigures his greater Son, Israel's Messiah (23).

The Gospel facts (27-32) cover the same details which are given in Peter's earlier addresses (**2**.22*ff*.; **3**.13.f; **10**.37-41), and the prophecies of Psalms **2** and **16** are again laid under tribute (33,35). Two prophecies are new. Which?

At the heart of his message lies the characteristic Pauline emphasis on (*i*) the resurrection of Jesus as God's vindication of Him, and (*ii*) the provision of righteousness by faith, which meets the demands of the Law. Verses 30 and 39 are pivotal; and *Romans* is the later elaboration of these vital themes.

Notes: V. 21: King Saul doesn't often figure in O.T. testimonies to Jesus. Did the speaker have a personal interest, coming from the same tribe (Phil. **3**.5)? V. 26: an appeal to born Jews and "God-fearers". V. 32: a favourite Pauline expression (Rom. **1**.16; 1 Cor. **9**.16).

To ponder: Neglect of spiritual truth is not always due to ignorance. Sometimes we can know it too well (27).

Acts 13.42-52

"Good news" (32) is meant to be shared. Many Jews and proselytes were won over and were encouraged to persevere (43). To judge from the next paragraph, they came back the next week with a great crowd of interested Gentiles (44,45). Did Paul see in this sequence a divine confirmation that this was Israel's destiny and mission—to be a light for the Gentiles (47)? National Israel—the Jewish people of old, represented in their synagogue officers of verse 45—had failed to seize this opportunity; the task therefore fell to the Christian apostles to accept the vocation of the servant and as "elect for the sake of mankind" to reach out to the distant peoples. So "we turn to the Gentiles" (46). This solemn announcement sounded the death-knell of Jewish exclusiveness and selfish particularism which said,

"What we have as a special privilege we want to keep to ourselves"'. It equally proved to be a manifesto and charter of Christian liberty and a promise of a worldwide Church. No longer could the Christian movement be thought of as a sect within Judaism—whatever misunderstanding their enemies might have; Acts **24.5** shows that this is what the Jews would like to have believed about the Church—but, having burst the cocoon, the missionary Church showed itself to be no inert chrysalis, but a living creature, ready to fly to earth's extremities with a message and a ministry to all (47). Small wonder that the Gentiles, regarded by official Judaism as beyond the pale and hopeless (Eph. **2.**1-3 picks up this sorry plight, but doesn't stop there), were overjoyed to receive the news of their salvation through Israel's Saviour.

Notes: V. 43: these converts are the God-fearers of v. 26 (see comment on **10.**2). V. 43: a follow-up ministry is intended, as at **11.**23. V. 46: "necessary" because of a priority stated in **3.**26; Rom. **1.**16; **11.**11*ff*., which Paul adhered to. But he refused to stay with obdurate Israel; he moved on to attend, in his own apostolic labours, to Israel's mission to the nations in the light of (*i*) his own call as apostle to the Gentiles (**22.**21), and (*ii*) the Servant prophecy of Isaiah **49.**6, with its primary application to Jesus but carried on by His people. V. 51: a symbolic action for a decisive break with human indifference (Mark **6.**11).

Acts 14.1-7

From Antioch the apostles moved on to Iconium, now called Konia, and a junction of several routes. Commentators draw attention to the Greek phrase (in v. 1) rendered "together". This should be translated "in the same way" with a backward glance at the apostolic procedure at Antioch. There the two apostles used the Jewish synagogue as a springboard for their evangelism; so too, in like manner, in spite of the declaration of **13.**46, they began their work at Iconium by visiting the Jewish assembly. A tiny word in verse 1, translated "so", speaks volumes of the way they conducted themselves. Their manner of life had a powerful effect in conjunction with the truth of their words.

Opposition also was encountered (2). Who were the "devil's advocates"? Which church in Asia Minor at a later time met this animosity from the Jews? (See Rev. **2.**8-11; and note the martyrdom of Polycarp which tells of Jewish opposition and evil designs in fomenting trouble for the Christians in the same place.) And in which other city did Paul feel encouraged to stay on because there was opposition to the work of the Gospel (as vs. 3, 4 imply)? (See **18.**6-11; 1 Cor. **16.**8,9).

A critical point was evidently reached when Paul learned of a concerted effort put in hand to attack him and his company (5,6). Then the principle of Matthew **10.**23 was invoked; and they took refuge in Lystra and Derbe, where fresh scope for evangelization was given (7).

Notes: V. 2: this disaffection was possibly caused by Jews who came on to Iconium from Antioch. Paul ignored their hostility (3), but felt it wise to move on when the local Gentile inhabitants seemed adamant in their resistance, even to the point of mob-violence (as verse 5 implies). V. 6: Lystra and Derbe, with the Phrygian city of Iconium, most probably (on Sir William Ramsay's view) represent the churches of Galatia to which the epistle of that name was written.

Study: Pick out some verses from Galatians which speak of the founding of the church in the teeth of hardship and opposition (e.g., Gal. 3.4) and with accompanying "signs and wonders" (e.g., Gal. 3.5).

Acts 14.8-18

Both parts of Paul's ministry at Lystra are full of interest. His action in healing the crippled man recalls Peter's work at the Temple gate (**3.**1—10). Both apostles evidently had a presence which commanded attention and drew out the earnest hopes of the needy invalids they encountered (note the double reference to intense longing—**3.**5 and **14.**9–which was matched by a direct look from the apostles).

The behaviour of the crowd (11-13) was typical of the people of Lycaonia whose district, so tradition reported, had once upon a time been favoured by a visit from Zeus (the king of the Greek gods) and Hermes (his messenger). Recent archaeological finds in that area of Asia Minor have shown that the cults of Zeus and Hermes flourished in the third century A.D. and go back earlier. In fact, the priests of Zeus (*cf.* v. 13) are referred to in the inscription unearthed by W. M. Calder of Manchester in 1922.

The second point of interest is Paul's speech (15-18). This brief and impromptu statement is the first opportunity Paul had to address a Gentile audience; and it is important to observe the features of the Christian message which it highlights. It cannot be complete in itself and was probably never finished, for Paul had still to mention the distinctive elements, such as the cross and resurrection of Jesus, when he was stopped (18). The verses, therefore, contain a preamble to the Gospel, and lay the foundation for it in a concise summary of "natural theology". What are the chief points which he makes (15-17)?

Notes: V. 9: how could this man's "faith to be made well" be evident to Paul? Was it a look in his eyes or any expression on his face? V. 11: the statement is at first not understood by Paul and Barnabas because of its strange language which they did not know; only when the Lystrans began to give them divine honours (13) did they realize the purport of it all. Hence their horrified rejection of what the people intended to do (14). V. 14: a sign of mourning: here it is expressive of disgust that the Lystrans should have regarded them as gods come to earth. Such actions were idolatry (15; 1 Thess. **1.**9), which is inexcusable in view of God's creatorship (15), past forbearance (16), and general revelation in Nature (Rom. **1.**19-23).

Further Study: Continue a comparison between Paul's experience with these people in Galatia and the letter he later wrote to them. For instance, see Galatians **4.**14 (*in the light of the name of Hermes given to him*); **1.**6; **3.**1 (*the Galatians' fickleness*); **6.**17 (*cf. verse* 19).

Acts 14.19-28

Experiences at Lystra left a permanent mark on Paul's mind (2 Tim. 3.11)—and his body, if Galatians **6.**17 is interpreted as the scars of his suffering in missionary service. Not for the last time did he face imminent death (19,20); and this successful attempt at rescue, as the disciples formed a ring around him, permitted him to escape, and, undeterred, to press on to the next town, Derbe.

Preaching and making disciples go hand in hand, according to the missionary manifesto of Matt. **28.**19, Mark **16.**15 (A.V.). The divine order and intention is that converts should become disciples. So it happened at Derbe (21).

"Tribulations" sounds an ominous note for the Church in every age and place; and there is no legitimate short-cut to avoid such a destiny. "Suffering, then, is the badge of the true Christian . . . Luther reckoned suffering among the marks of the true Church, and one of the memoranda drawn up in preparation for the Augsburg Confession similarly defines the Church as the community of those "who are persecuted and martyred for the Gospel's sake" . . . "Discipleship means allegiance to the suffering Christ" (Bonhoeffer).

Further pastoral provision was made in the appointment of a simple church leadership (23). What was the prime responsibility of these "elders" (see **20.**28; Titus **1.**5-9; 1 Tim. **3.**1-7)?

Vs. 24-28 complete the story of the missionary circuit. Paul and his party return to the place from which they were valedicted (26). *Notes:* V. 19: Paul's stoning is part of his apostolic hardships recorded in 2 Corinthians **11.**25. Note the sudden change in the Galatians—from enthusiastic hero-worship to a bitter attack on Paul's person. V. 22: a pastoral follow-up is indicated in the verbs (*cf.* **18.**23 and **11.**23; **13.**43). The key-verb is "must"—not an optional vocation which may be bypassed. Similarly, 2 Tim. **2.**3; **3.**12; Rev. **7.**14. V. 23: "elders" represent an oversight of the local congregation, as at Ephesus (Acts **20.**17) and Philippi (Phil. **1.**1). Other functions are given in Romans **12.**8; 1 Thessalonians **5.**12; Hebrews **13.**17. V. 27: indeed an "open door" (Rev. **3.**8). Where else did Paul use this metaphor for a ready scope for the Gospel? *To think over: Look back over Paul's provision for the new converts—in verses 22 and 23. Are we sufficiently attentive to such needs?*

Acts 15.1-5

The immediate occasion of the Council was the success which attended Paul's missionary journey. Jews and Jewish proselytes had been won, but, more significantly, the Gospel had made a noticeable inroad into pagan territory and (chiefly in Galatia) a ready welcome to the message had been received. So much so that Paul had introduced a rudimentary church organization for the maintaining of congregational life and growth (**14.**22,23). News of this had reached the Jerusalem church, where alarm was felt. Why?

The "dissension and debate" centred on the admissibility of Gentile believers to the Church. Cornelius was clearly a special case, and at all events, he was half-way to becoming a Jew before his conversion to Christ. The issue was whether Gentile converts were to be welcomed *en masse* the moment they were converted—or to be gradually introduced to full Christian standing by receiving the imposition of certain Jewish rites and rituals. Note the chief qualification which the strict Jewish Christians were insisting upon (1).

The danger of a divided Church, split into two factions and with two headquarters, at Jerusalem and at Antioch, was present. So to settle the question (2) a consultation was arranged. Clearly Paul and Barnabas stood for a liberal attitude, which Paul strenuously argues for in his Galatian epistle; while at the opposite end of the scale, a rigid policy of turning Gentile converts into good Jews before according them a full Christian status was adopted. *Who were the spokesmen for this line* (5)?

Notes: V. 2: the precise relation between this visit and an earlier one (**11**.30) in the light of Galatians **2**.1-10 is much canvassed. The simplest solution is that the Galatians **2** visit is the same as that of **11**.30, and that the letter to the Galatians was written *before* this council in A.D. 49. This explains why there is no reference to the decree in Galatians. It is less easy to account for its omission from 1 Corinthians. Probably Paul accepted it in principle, but based his appeal to the Corinthians on other grounds (1 Cor. **8**; *cf.* Rom. **14**.1—**15**.6). V. 3: Paul evidently enlisted much sympathy, including Luke's. V. 5: this restriction was intolerable, and a betrayal of the Gospel of God's free grace, according to Paul's (earlier) letter to Galatia. Why?

Acts 15.6-12

Much debate evidently led nowhere (7); and Peter's statement was intended to cut through the knot by an assertion that the grace of the Lord Jesus was the sole requirement for salvation (11).

His rehearsal of God's dealings with him served to underscore the important points of conviction: (*i*) God Himself had taken the initiative in the choosing and calling of Cornelius (7); (*ii*) the proof of His pleasure was the giving of the Holy Spirit in the same way and on the same basis as the blessing of Pentecost which inaugurated the Christian era (8, 9); (*iii*) as there was no distinction in the gift of Messianic grace, there must be no "extra" necessity which would obscure the gracious way in which God chooses to act (9, 11); and (*iv*) in any case, to insist on a Jewish prescription is an invitation to bondage from which Christ has set us free (10). Which verse, with its ringing tones of freedom in Christ, in *Galatians* does this echo?

Peter had profited from the rebuke administered by Paul at Antioch (Gal. **2**.11-21). At that earlier time he had vacillated by, at first, welcoming the Gentiles as brothers and sharers in a common table; but later, when put under pressure, he had "played the Pharisee" (Gal. **2**.12a) by a deliberate withdrawal and refusal to share fellowship. Note his motivation then (Gal. **2**.12b). And its effect on others. What exactly was at stake in Antioch?

Notes: V. 7: "early days"—the Cornelius episode happened some ten years before. The divine "choice" recalls the election of Abraham

(Neh. **9**.7); Cornelius is the firstfruits of a new people of God. V. 9: "cleansed", as in **10**.15; **11**.9. V. 10: "a yoke upon the neck" re-echoes a familiar Jewish phrase ("to take up the yoke of the kingdom of heaven") for accepting the Jewish religion. Peter here reflects the attitude of Galilean Jews to the burdensome regulations of Pharisaism. Jesus too offered release from this heavy "yoke" (Matt. **11**.29, 30; *cf.* Matt. 23.4; Luke **11**.46). V. 11: a clear statement of free grace, unencumbered by any "works", of which Paul would not have been ashamed.

Meditation: In a day when theological discussion and debate get more and more complicated, let us ponder the apostolic declaration (11) with its note of (i) impressive simplicity—"the grace of the Lord Jesus"; (ii) triumphant certainty—"we believe . . . that we shall be saved"; and (iii) unconfined universality—"we . . . as . . . they".

Acts 15.13-21

It is James' turn to contribute to the discussion. He expresses cordial acceptance of Peter's statement (14: Symeon is Peter's first name, John **1**.40-42) by discovering a Scriptural precedent for the thought that God intended to include the Gentiles in the assembling of His people. This is part of the missionary message of the Old Testament.

The quotation from Amos **9**.11*f.* is taken from the Greek Old Testament and makes two points: (*i*) the rebuilding of David's dwelling (16 in James's speech) speaks of God's covenant of restoration with Israel after the exile. This is now fulfilled in Messiah's coming to His people; (*ii*) verse 17 relates to "the rest of men"—*i.e.*, the Gentiles who are called by God's Name—and the promise is that they too find a place within the fold of God's people. The upshot is the statement of verse 19, which is a clear counter-statement of the Judaizing proposals of verses 1 and 5.

One consideration of a practical nature required some attention, however. Exactly what this is depends upon how we construe verses 20 and 21—the text of the so-called "apostolic decree". In the R.S.V. there are four items of "prohibited practices", all of them having to do with practices which mean much to orthodox Jews—*viz.*, idolatry, immorality, eating meat from animals which had been improperly (by Rabbinic standards) slaughtered—*i.e.*, by being strangled, and from animals which still retained the blood. If these prohibitions were imposed on Gentile believers, the intention will have been to make possible table-fellowship between Jewish and Gentile Christians. If the latter would accept this code, the former would not be scandalized.

The difficulty with this reconstruction is that in Paul's dealings with Gentile churches (at Rôme and Corinth) he refuses to legislate in this formal way and leaves the question of "unclean foods" to be settled by considerations of conscience (see I.V.F. *New Bible Dictionary*, "Idols, meat offered to"). The R.S.V. margin, which adopts the "Western text", may, therefore, be preferred. Then, with the omission of a reference to what is strangled, the remaining *three* items may be taken as parts of an ethical code, *viz.*, idolatry, adultery (probably by marriage within the prohibited degrees of Leviticus **18**), and bloodshed (=murder). Paul would have had no scruple about accepting such elementary moral regulations for Gentile believers, whereas his "fight for Galatia", already won, is not likely to have been thrown away by his tamely accepting some ceremonial rules (on the R.S.V. text reading). Therefore we may prefer the R.S.V. margin; and Church practice in the second century confirms this.

Acts 15.22-35

A delegation of four men is appointed to carry this letter containing the terms of the "apostolic decree" from Jerusalem to Antioch. It was at Antioch that Christian fellowship between the two branches of the Church had been disrupted by the arrival of certain Jerusalem teachers (called Judaizers) who, claiming to speak with James's authority, insisted on a separation of Jewish Christians from uncircumcised Gentile believers, and brought pressure to bear upon Peter (Gal. 2.11*ff*.). It was therefore necessary that (*i*) these Judaizers should be checked (24); (*ii*) Paul and Barnabas who had put matters right at Antioch should be vindicated by the general assembly (25,26); (*iii*) some independent evidence of the assembly's decision should be provided, lest the Antiochians should imagine that Paul was inventing all this. Two impartial witnesses are commended (27); and it was further required that (*iv*) the terms of Christian moral practices should be spelled out clearly, so that the high moral tone of the Church which was quickly becoming the spiritual home of Gentiles who were converted to Christ from a world of licence, immorality, and self-indulgence should be preserved (28,29). The guidance of the Holy Spirit is acknowledged in this epoch-making decision (28).

How was the decree received (31)? Further explanations were given by the two accredited delegates, who had a spiritual gift of prophecy (*cf*. 1 Cor. **14**.3).

Notes: V. 22: Judas Barsabbas—was he brother to Joseph Barsabbas (**1.**23)? Silas (or Silvanus) is first introduced. He played an important part in the Pauline and Petrine correspondence (1 Thess. **1.**1; 2 Thess. **1.**1; 2 Cor. **1.**19; 1 Pet. **5.**12). V. 24: "unsettling your minds"— a military term for plundering a town. V. 26: "risked"—the Greek verb is the same as Galatians **2.**20; Romans **4.**25; **8.**32. Perhaps we should translate: "men who have dedicated their lives". But the R.S.V. thought recurs in Philippians **2.**30. V. 33: "in peace"=with the good wishes of the congregation, and in prospect of Silas' return to Antioch (40; v. 34 in the margin simply confuses).

Question: "The Acts of the Holy Spirit" is one apt description of this book. Here we see His guidance in the business and decisions of a church assembly (25, 28). *How shall we make provision for Him to lead our denominational and united Church conferences today?*

Acts 15.36-41

Six verses which offer a fascinating study in early Church personalities!

Paul and Barnabas both agreed that it was opportune to re-visit the churches of Galatia (36); but that was as far as the *entente* went. Both men had different opinions of John Mark, who had accompanied them on the earlier journey, but had retired somewhat unceremoniously (**13.**13) at what proved to be only the outset of the tour. The result was a distressing situation—Luke calls it by a strong name, an altercation (Greek, *paroxysmos*, 39) which could only be settled by the two men going their several ways.

Who was right? Probably both men were right—up to a point. Paul, no mean judge of men, saw that Mark's character at that time was not suited to the strains and stresses of another missionary journey (considering the importance of this venture in the light of the council's ruling and the need to press onwards resolutely into the heart of the Greco-Roman world with the Gospel). Barnabas, on the other hand, was prepared to overlook one lapse in the hope of a stronger character yet to emerge, and perhaps the axiom "blood's thicker than water" controlled his decision to give his relative a second chance.

At all events, two happier notes are struck in the later story. First, by a division of labour, *two* missionary parties set out and so more territory was evangelized. Secondly, "all's well that ends well", and the final chapter in Mark's story is that of a recovery. "Failure is not final" (E. M. Blaiklock)—see 2 Tim. **4.**11, with its glowing

tribute to Mark's usefulness at the last; 1 Pet. **5.**13 for Peter's special interest; and, of course, the Gospel of Mark—
> The saint who first found grace to pen
> The Life which was the light of men.

Notes: Vs. 37,38: the commentators draw attention to a subtle change in the tenses here. Barnabas wanted to decide *to take* (aorist, implying a single action), but Paul foresaw the risk of having *to take* Mark as a continual partner (present tense)— and liable at any moment to desert them. V. 40: Silas was admirably qualified as a Jerusalem Christian and a Roman citizen (**16.**37*ff.*).

To think over: "*An unedifying episode*". Yes, but are there no redeeming features?

Acts 16.1-5

Paul received some compensation for the indignity he suffered on his first visit to Lystra (**14.**19,20). At least one convert had gone on in the life of the Spirit—and so was ready for the touch of God upon him. He was Timothy. Notice some points of special commendation: (*i*) His progress since his conversion is perhaps indicated in the name "disciple" (1)—*i.e.*, learner and student in the school of Christ. He had matured to that extent. Who, elsewhere in the New Testament, had failed to grow in the Christian life (Heb. **5.**11-14)? (*ii*) Verse 2 is an important feature to be observed in any young person who feels the call of God to full-time service. Timothy had a good reputation, and was *persona grata* with the leaders of the neighbouring churches. The reason for this character reference is given in 1 Tim. **4.**12. (*iii*) The will of God was made known to Timothy by the agency of Paul, who addressed to him the summons to divine service (3a). The apostle must have been able to perceive in him the makings of a real man of God; and he was not disappointed.

Two subsequent developments confirmed the correctness and wisdom of Paul's choice. First, Paul was able to send Timothy more than once as his personal representative—and almost as an extension of his own personality—to the churches (1 Cor. **4.**17; Phil. **2.**19-24; 1 Thess. **3.**2). And, at the last hour of his life, Paul requested Timothy's presence (2 Tim. **4.**9,21).

The mention of Timothy's circumcision comes as a surprise in view of the apostolic decree (referred to again in verse 4). But there were evidently special circumstances to be respected—*viz.*, Timothy was a half-Jew already (1), and Paul simply "regularized his status"

(F. F. Bruce) in having him circumcised. Besides, the question of salvation was not in view here, as in the Galatian churches at the time of the (earlier) Judaizing controversy. Then, the avoidance of circumcision was a prime requirement (Gal. 5.2,11). Does 1 Cor. 9. 19-23 bear upon this distinction?

Notes: V. 1: mixed marriages, then as now, create a problem, and not least for the children. In Jewish eyes Timothy would be regarded as illegitimate—hence Paul's desire to remove the stigma by this minor surgical operation. And this would be important if Timothy's future ministry were to be acceptable to the Jews for whose salvation Paul still yearned (Rom. 9.3; 10.1). On Timothy's Jewish ancestry, see 2 Tim. 1.5.

Questions: Are we (i) as ready as Paul was to encourage young people in the Lord's service? (ii) as alert as Timothy was to respond to His call through older Christians?

Acts 16.6-10

There are some points of particular interest in this passage: (*i*) The ministry of the Holy Spirit is seen here in both restraining (6,7) and constraining the Christian missionaries. The verbs used indicate clearly the Spirit's personality and His intimate association with the person of Jesus (especially verse 7: a unique description, but it is hinted at in John 14.16). (*ii*) Guidance came in the form of a human voice, heard in Paul's night-time vision. The circumstances of this encounter with the Macedonian "man" whom Sir William Ramsay suggested was Luke himself, and the clear direction given in the call to cross over the Aegean sea, led Paul to the firm conviction that this was the guidance he sought. In fact, he needed such guidance, because the way ahead was blocked. Why? (*iii*) At this point in the narrative the literary form changes, and verse 10 introduces a new, unheard-of feature in Luke's history. Can you spot it?

Few sections of the Bible hold such useful teaching on the theme of guidance. Re-read the passage in the light of the following suggestions: (*i*) We may confidently expect a guided life as the children of God. He will direct us *away* from the second-best, if we are faced with a choice; (*ii*) He may lead us through some fellow-believer, some "man of Macedonia" whose word comes to our prepared and responsive minds; but we must cultivate a sensitivity to *hear*; (*iii*) when circumstances combine to indicate a course of action, we are expected to use a God-given faculty of common sense and perception (10).

Notes: V. 6: the "South Galatian" view interprets this phrase as meaning the region of *Phrygia Galatica*, evangelized by Paul on his earlier journey (**13.14***ff.*) and inhabited by the readers addressed in the epistle to the Galatians. Paul was checked from turning west towards Ephesus (6) and north-eastward into Bithynia (7). V. 9: the first extended "we" section, indicating the presence of Luke. V. 10: the verb normally means "to put together" (*cf.* our colloquial "putting two and two together"—*i.e.*, concluding.)

Acts 16.11-24

Philippi had two claims to fame (12). What were they? A more illustrious and enduring claim was begun on the day of Paul's arrival, for this city was honoured as the first "European" city to hear and to receive the good news of God. Perhaps this thought lies behind Philippians **1.**5; **4.**15. Two notable conversions are described:

(*i*) *Vs. 13-15.* Lydia hailed from Thyatira, a centre of the dyeing trade in Asia Minor. She was evidently on business in Philippi, and had some attachment to the Jewish faith as a God-fearer.

Her conviction illustrates what the theologians call "prevenient grace"—*i.e.*, that God took the initiative, "went before", in her readiness to hear the word by pre-disposing her to give a ready acceptance to the Saviour's call (14b). Notice her confession of faith in baptism and her gracious, if firm, offer of hospitality. Perhaps Paul was unwilling to accept the hospitality, but she had her way (15b) as the first convert in Europe. If Lydia is an example to follow, which other woman of Thyatira gives a warning to avoid (Rev. **2.**18-20)?

(*ii*) *Vs. 16-24* remind us that the world of Paul's day was peopled by men and women who made a living out of religious humbug and chicanery. The girl fortune-teller found release from her spiritual bondage "in the Name of Jesus Christ" (18). On a quickly-invented charge Paul and Silas fell victim to her masters' annoyance at the loss of their profits, the crowd's venom, and the magistrates' indifference to elementary justice. Even the jailer seemed hostile, as he placed his prisoners' legs in the torturing stocks. But their deliverance—and his too—was shortly to appear!

Notes: V. 12: "a Roman colony"—see Phil. **1.**27; **3.**20 for the use Paul makes of this fact. V. 13: a prayer-meeting in the open air. V. 17: the girl perceives that these are "holy men" offering a spiritual message. V. 20: Luke is accurate with his term for the magistrates, *praetores duoviri.*

Acts 16.25-34

Three miracles disturbed the citizens of Philippi during the day and night when they presumed to place the Christian preachers in their local jail:

(*i*) The first miracle is in the realm of the human spirit, which, renewed and fortified by Christ, rises above the grim and painful experiences of the prisoners' cell and the instrument of torture, and finds a song of praise to God (25). Paul and his companion took their adverse circumstances as a challenge to faith (Rom. **8**.28); a clarion call to victory (Rom. **5**.17; 2 Cor. **2**.14); and a springboard for witness (25b). Many a man would have cursed his luck, renounced his gods, and tried to bribe the jailer; Paul found a better outlet for his pent-up feelings (Phil. **4**.6,7).

(*ii*) The earthquake came at the right time and for precisely the required purpose—to release the prisoners from their chains and to open the cell doors, but not to destroy life. Moreover, the supernatural disturbance struck terror into the jailer's heart, giving him a salutary fear and anxious concern for "salvation" (30).

(*iii*) Terror betrays a bad conscience, which in turn stems from disharmony with God because of sin. Therefore, all need is comprehended in man's first requirement—to know God as Saviour, which stamps Christ's Gospel as uniquely suited to that need (31). Here is the miracle of grace, as the jailer passes from death to life (Col. **1**.13, 14), with his family, from the solitude of alienation and fear into the joyous family of God (33,34).

The apostles' "joy in suffering", the phenomenon wholly from God, and the wonder of the simple Gospel—these marked out the establishment of the Philippian church as God's "good work" (Phil. **1**.6). Is there anywhere a nobler work?

Notes: V. 25: an O.T. psalm or a Christian canticle. V. 26: the moorings of the prisoners' fetters fixed to the wall became loose (Ramsay). V. 27: suicide would vindicate his military honour, and avoid the reproach of having failed in his duty. V. 30: perhaps he had heard the slave-girl's cry (17). V. 33: note the two uses of water. Sacrament and service go together.

Acts 16.35-40

Why did the magistrates change their minds and send the policeman to discharge the prisoners (35)? And why did Paul refuse to accept his freedom in this way (37)? Was it a fit of pique which made him disgruntled? Or a desire to see justice done by demanding a full apology? Or (more likely) an insistence on an official release and admission of error so that there would be no recurrence of this kind of hindrance to his missionary labours?

Anyhow, he acted clearly within his civil rights and got what he demanded even to the full apology and regret that they had blundered into beating and imprisoning Roman citizens whose case had not been investigated (37).

There are some pointers here to aid our thinking about the Christian's civil and social responsibility. Notice how Paul and Silas stand for their civic rights (Rom. **13.**1*ff*.), yet, once they have attained their aim, they comply with lawful authority and refuse to be an "odd ball" or social misfit (1 Pet. **2.**13-17).

Notes: V. 35: the accurate terminology is again to be seen. The "praetors" send their "lictors" (lit. rod-bearers) who carried as a badge of office bundles of rods bound together round an axe. V. 37: Paul uses the technical term "uncondemned" (*re incognita*, "without investigating the case")—a monstrous crime against Roman citizens, though not without precedent. Paul and Silas (37: "us") may have claimed their exemption from punishment on the previous day, but have been shouted down by the mob (22). V. 39: a noticeable change of face from v. 35. V. 40: Lydia's home was possibly the church's meeting-place, and housed a virile and affectionate company of believers to whom Paul became specially attached. Read his letter to the Philippians, detecting its warm, pastoral tones.

To think over: "*One cannot help feeling that this is the best story Luke has given us so far*" (*Findlay*). *Do you agree?*

Acts 17.1-9

The apostolic band (minus Luke, who evidently stayed on at Philippi to consolidate the work there; the "we-narrative" abruptly breaks off at **16.**17) moved southward, calling at Amphipolis (30 miles from Philippi) and Apollonia (27 miles further on) *en route* to Thessalonica (another 35 miles). The excellent Roman roads—this one was the useful *via Egnatia*—made travel both safe and speedy, and both factors were of incalculable importance for the spread of the Gospel message in the early days of the Church.

At Thessalonica a three weeks' ministry at the local Jewish meeting-place (2) gave Paul a chance to set out the Scriptural basis of his message. Note the three chief emphases he made (3). The reaction was true to previous experience. Some were convinced and won over to faith in Jesus as Messiah and Lord; this response angered the Jews, who raised the rabble against the visiting missionaries on the handy charge that they preached a subversive message which called for disloyalty to Rome (6,7). The evidence for this accusation was the proclamation of the Kingship of Jesus, which the Jews interpreted in a malicious way to mean that the Christian preachers were political agitators, offering a rival emperor to Caesar. The authorities, however, were not easily taken in by this specious allegation, but did investigate the claim. Jason, at whose house the apostles were lodging, was required to give an assurance that his guests were not seditiously-minded (9); and to make sure, Jason agreed that the apostles should be "bound over" and prevented from speaking in Thessalonica. This explains their immediate departure for Beroea (10).

Notes: V. 2: R.S.V. margin gives "sabbaths" as an alternative translation. On successive sabbath days Paul was the invited preacher. Perhaps the three themes (of v. 3) were handled on these consecutive sabbaths. V. 4: the adherence of some influential women reminds us that Christian ladies play a significant part in early Church life. Which names come to mind? Priscilla, Phoebe, Lydia . . . Turn up Romans **16** for many more. V. 5: the "loafers" (lit. those who hang about the market-place). V. 5: Paul was not there when Jason's house was attacked.

Meditation: "*These men have turned the world upside down*" (6). *Christian preaching is not a sedative, but social and spiritual dynamite.*

Acts 17.10-15

We have Paul's later comment on the turn of events which made him rather suddenly have to quit Thessalonica (1 Thess. **2.**18). Possibly he would not have accepted the dismissal so tamely, but Jason had given his word to the magistrates (9) and he would abide by that.

So he came to Beroea, 60 miles away. Here the previous pattern of his ministry was repeated. His preaching was evidently conducted in no "take-it-or-leave-it" manner, for it encouraged people to investigate the Scriptures for themselves. Not surprisingly, when this happens, "many of them . . . believed" (12). Truth, personally sought out and discovered by us, is always more vital and dear than thoughts which are handed to us "on a plate".

Meanwhile, the infant church at Thessalonica was facing much hardship (see 1 Thess. **1.**6; **2.**14; **3.**3) and yet it did not cease its witness to the Gospel (1 Thess. **1.**8). A later reference in that letter implies that persecution had caused the premature death of some believers (1 Thess. **4.**13); and the Jewish leaders, determined to crush every outcropping of the Church, moved on to Beroea (13).

Paul had to face fresh opposition from the Thessalonian Jews, and felt it wise to travel on to Athens, using Silas and Timothy as his delegates to encourage the believers in the place he had been forced to flee (15). So much is clear; but it is very likely (from 1 Thess.) that Paul had to meet another kind of insinuation. Perhaps he had been accused of cowardice and running away from danger; or of double-dealing, by staying at Thessalonica only long enough to get a money-gift from Philippi, and then quickly moving on, hoping to collect more subscriptions from rich ladies *en route*. So he seeks to vindicate his character and to account for his actions in the Thessalonian letters. And, to make matters worse, he couldn't come in person to Thessalonica while the promise and pledge given by Jason were still in force. So he sent two men as his personal representatives.

Notes: V. 11: "noble"—in their attitude to the message? Yet Paul never hints at a defect in Thessalonica. The Greek can mean "more generous": can it refer to their support of the missionaries by gifts? Hence the defence (in 1 Thess. **2.**5,9,10) of being disinterested and above-board. V. 14: *cf.* 1 Thess. 3.1*ff*.

Acts 17.16-21

The apostle's first reaction to what he saw at Athens led to a public ministry of disputation, both in the Jewish synagogue and in the market-place. No record is given of his appreciation of the city's objects of beauty; what fastened itself on his mind was its senseless idolatry (16)—a judgment called forth by the excessive religiosity of the Athenians (22) and their custom of dedicating shrines to a variety of deities (23).

There are two settings of his encounter with the philosophers who met him. In the market-place they overheard his preaching, which they couldn't understand. To their ears he kept on referring to "Jesus and the resurrection" (18), which they probably misconstrued as an allusion to two deities: Jesus and His consort *Anastasis* (the Greek word for resurrection). Others seemed to have dismissed him with the disdainful term "babbler" (lit. seed-picker, a slang expression for a worthless person who picked up scraps of food in the markets). But some wished to hear more.

The second scene is the Areopagus (19), a venue for the Athenian court and a meeting-point for religious discussion and debate. Luke evidently had a pretty poor opinion of the value of what usually went on there (21); and his verdict was not unshared.

Notes: V. 16: Athens, the cultural centre of the Greco-Roman world, renowned for the sculpture of Pheidias. But Paul's spirit was provoked by its idols. The verb occurs in the Old Testament for God's anger at Israel's apostasy (Deut. **9.**18; Psa. **106.**29). V. 18: these two groups held beliefs which Paul touches upon in his sermon, *viz.,*—the Epicurean notion that God is all-sufficient in Himself; and the Stoic doctrine that He gives life to all (*cf.* v. 25). The word "preacher" means "herald" and was a technical expression in the Greek mystery religions. A different term is used at Romans **10.**14. Vs. 19,20: "new teaching", "strange things"; *cf.* the reaction to our Lord's ministry (Mark **1.**27; Luke **5.**26), but for different reasons. Why? V. 21: Demosthenes, the Greek orator, had accused his fellow-Athenians of "going round and asking, Is anything new being said?" This is a human trait in every age, based on the false assumption that the latest vogue is the best. Theologians are not exempt.

Acts 17.22-34

Paul's apologetic or defence of the faith before the Athenians is a classic statement of "natural theology". An earlier and shorter specimen was given at **14.**15-17. It aims at laying a foundation on which the special revelation of the Gospel may be built; but no foundation is ever complete in itself and requires a superstructure to explain its *raison d'être*. Paul, taking his text from an altar reared to an "Unknown god" (23), proceeds to state the answer to the basic question of all theology, Who is God?

(*i*) He is Maker, Lord of heaven and earth (24); (*ii*) who is Spirit, unimprisoned in any earthly temple (25,29; John **4.**24); (*iii*) He is self-existent, in whom all creation lives (25). This answers the children's insistent question, "Who made God?" (*iv*) He is Creator of men, whose span of life and dwelling-place on earth are determined by Him (26). If the last phrase of verse 26 refers to territorial ambitions, then God is seen as Lord of history, concerned with the rise and fall of national powers; (*v*) moreover, He is the source and goal of man's spiritual life (27,28).

Two final attributes (30,31) are logically connected with this list. As God is One and almighty, with no visible image, all idolatry stands under His judgment since He is a righteous Lord who summons men to repentance. As Lord of history and of the Universe, it is His design to bring the world to its consummation at the final day of reckoning. The proof of this final judgment has been given in Jesus' resurrection from the dead.

Paul's hearers would follow him in the preliminary stages of his case, but mention of repentance (which implies sin), judgment (which involves moral responsibility), and the resurrection and return of Jesus (which ran counter to all Greek ideas of immortality and union with God) was too much for most of them. Some derided (32); some deferred (32); only a few decided for the Pauline Gospel (34). Had Paul failed in this situation?

Notes: V. 23: there is independent evidence of altars at Athens "to unknown gods" set up in time of civic distress, and as a feature of man's incurable religiosity (22). Paul accepts this as a fact of experience (27), confirmed by man's being created by God in His image (28). V. 28: a quotation from Aratus, and an allusion to a line in Cleanthes—both Stoic poets. Aratus hailed from Paul's place of origin. V. 30: *cf.* Rom. **3.**25*f.*

Meditation: Universal kinship with Adam (26) and the world's future judgment by the last Adam (31)—these are the terminal points of the sermon, and of Christian doctrine today.

Acts 18.1-4

When he later reflected on his ministry in this part of southern Greece, Paul wrote of "the household of Stephanas" as the first converts in Achaia (1 Cor. **16.**15)—and Stephanas was a Corinthian. This suggests that no church—certainly no thriving community—was left in Athens after his departure.

Some scholars infer that, on reflection, Paul regretted the philosophical and cultural approach which he made to the Athenians, and that 1 Corinthians **2.**1-5 was written out of a new resolve henceforth to focus his preaching on "Jesus Christ and Him crucified". We may doubt this inference, but it does seem clear that, in direct contrast to a somewhat barren ministry in Athens, the initial response at Corinth was a tremendous encouragement to him. In fact, from his letters, the evidence is that the church at Corinth turned out to be his main pastoral concern.

The exigencies of the situation at Corinth also may have contributed to his desire to proclaim the "simple Gospel" in full reliance on the Holy Spirit. For Corinth was a flourishing seaport, notorious for its moral laxity and crude ways, the "Vanity Fair" of the Roman Empire. The verb in Greek "to corinthianize" means "to go to the dogs"!

In such an unpromising setting Paul directed his ministry to both Jews and Greeks (4), and found support in two friends, husband and wife, who had been forced out of Italy by an imperial edict aimed at the Jews (c. A.D.49-50). Jewish rabbis were taught a trade, so it is not surprising to read this reference to Paul's craftsmanship (3).

Notes: V. 2: these two Christians play a significant, if secondary, role in the New Testament literature. Paul was later to owe much to them (Rom. **16.**3,4; *cf.* 1 Cor. **16.**19; 2 Tim. **4.**19). The decree of Claudius is that mentioned by the historian Suetonius. V. 3: the trade was that of leather-working. Paul's occupation to support his ministry is well attested (*cf.* **20.**34; 1 Cor. **9.**12,15; 2 Cor. **11.**7*ff.*; 1 Thess. **2.**9; 2 Thess. **3.**8).

Question: Consider the apostle's example at Corinth and its bearing on (i) lay ministry, and (ii) part-time pastoral ministry.

Acts 18.5-11

We may pick out a number of features of Paul's labours at Corinth:

(*i*) His evangelism. Verse 5 reads, "Paul was engrossed in this preaching of the word" (Moffatt) once Silas and Timothy arrived. Probably their coming and work freed him from the necessity of dividing his time between preaching and his craft, and made a full-time ministry possible.

(*ii*) His decision, following on the hardened attitude of the Jews (6,7), to divert his energies into the channel of a mission to the Gentiles (8) and to set up a rival meeting-place next door to the synagogue. Would this arrangement have been approved by modern missionary policy-makers? But Crispus' conversion seems to have been a direct fruit of this bold venture, to be followed by that of many Corinthians.

(*iii*) His encouragement (9,10). In spite of some success and the strength of Christian fellowship in the work, Paul grew depressed, and needed the enheartening reminder and caution of a night-time vision. The message is precisely suited to his immediate situation: "Stop being afraid, and go on speaking". A special promise of the Lord's protecting hand implies that his life was in some peril; and the assurance that his work was not to be in vain (1 Cor. **15.**58) must have breathed fresh courage into his jaded spirit. (Compare 1 Kings **19.**18.) The effect on Paul was notable (11).

Notes: V. 5: perhaps Silas and Timothy brought him gifts from the Macedonian churches (2 Cor. **11.**8; Phil. **4.**15) and this made possible a full-time ministry. V. 6: "he shook out his garments"—an act of protest (*cf.* Neh. **5.**13). For the following phrase, see Matt. **27.**25. V. 7: Ramsay identifies this man with Gaius (Rom. **16.**23). What we do know is that he was a Roman citizen and a God-fearer. V. 8: Paul refers to this conversion in 1 Corinthians **1.**14 (baptism following conversion) and Gaius (?Titius Justus) is mentioned there also. V. 9: notice the translation above, which brings out the Greek tenses. Something of Paul's fear is reflected in 1 Corinthians **2.**3. For the Church as God's people, see 1 Peter **2.**9,10.

Acts 18.12-23

Vs. 12-17 give details of the kind of opposition which Paul met at Corinth (10), and his policy of setting up a rival centre next door to the Jewish synagogue led, not unnaturally, to this "united attack" on him. He was haled before the tribunal of Gallio, who was proconsul of Achaia in A.D.51. In his capacity as local magistrate, Gallio heard the charge (13), but did not stay for the defendant's reply (14). He just couldn't be bothered, as verse 17 implies, even when a flagrant injustice was done before his eyes.

Vs. 18-23. Paul's itinerary took him from Corinth *via* Ephesus to Antioch, and then back to Galatia to re-visit the churches in that province. At Ephesus he parted company with Aquila and his wife (26; and in 1 Cor. **16.**19, written from Ephesus, he conveys a greeting from them to their friends at Corinth). The allusion to a vow (18) is interesting. Based on Num. **6.**1-21, the custom of taking a Nazirite vow was followed by a man before setting out on a dangerous journey. The traveller would vow not to cut his hair until the trip was completed; then he would shear his head at a ceremony of thanksgiving in the Jerusalem Temple (**21.**23,24). It was Paul's intention, once his hair was cut at Cenchreae, not to have it cut again until he reached Jerusalem in safety. Then the hair would be offered as a token of thankfulness for "journeying mercies". Probbably we may understand a visit to Jerusalem in the phrase "went up" (22). This is Luke's ending of the second missionary tour, the final stage being told with breathless rapidity.

Notes: V. 12: Gallio was the brother of the famous philosopher Seneca, who in turn was a tutor of Nero. V. 13: it is not certain what this accusation means; whose law is Paul supposedly contravening, Jewish or Roman? Gallio replies that on both counts Paul is no criminal, as far as he can see. He clears Paul of breaking a Roman law, and professes no interest in the domestic issue of Jewish affairs. V. 17: Sosthenes may be the same as in 1 Corinthians **1.**1. If so, he too (like Crispus, 8) may have then been converted, and the Jews show their anger at losing *two* leaders to the Christian cause. But it may have been *Greeks* who gave Sosthenes a beating, taking advantage of Gallio's unconcern (so the Western text). V. 22*f.*: "in these two verses and **19.**1 is compressed a journey of 1,500 miles" (F. F. Bruce).

Acts 18.24-28

Apollos' gifts were considerable: (*i*) "learning", by which we are probably to understand a gift of public speaking—*i.e.*, eloquence (24); (*ii*) a close acquaintance with the Old Testament Scriptures, which he used in a ministry to the synagogues (26); and (*iii*) an ardour (25) which drove him to share with others the knowledge he had of Jesus. Something of the infectiousness of his zeal is hinted at in this memorable description: "fervent in spirit", or perhaps, "bubbling over with enthusiasm" (*cf.* Rom. **12.**11 for the same phrase). Yet he possessed a commendable trait which must have endeared him to all; his humility and teachableness which did not refuse to accept fuller instruction of "the way of God" (26). The maxim of Prov. **9.**9 sums it up.

Following this "course of instruction" which Priscilla and Aquila (note the order of names) gave him at Ephesus, there was an increase in Apollos's influence as he crossed over the Aegean sea to southern Greece. Here he was welcomed, and exercised a two-sided ministry. He stimulated and strengthened the believers (27), probably at Corinth (where unhappily his name became associated with a clique in the church, 1 Cor. **1.**12; **3.**4,22). Incidentally Paul pays a warm tribute to his work at Corinth (1 Cor. **3.**6: "Apollos watered" the spiritual shoots and slips planted by the apostle). Then, he conducted a public campaign of "Christian evidences" against the denials and contradictions of the Jews (28).

Notes: V. 24: Apollos' culture derived from the advantage of living at Alexandria, the Sorbonne of the ancient world, famed for its library and letters. Apollos' knowledge of the O.T. would be that of the Septuagint version, and his religious experience seems to have been that of a pre-Pentecostal nature. Possibly he was a member of a group which venerated John the Baptist, although recognizing the existence of Jesus' Messiahship and an experimental knowledge of the Holy Spirit (see on ch. **19**). This explains the effectiveness of his later ministry, based on his ready aptitude to learn (28). V. 27: a "letter of commendation" is meant, like those referred to in 2 Corinthians **3.1**.

Question: To be a leader, without becoming a party-leader, is not easy. How does Paul deal with factions at Corinth (1 *Cor.* **1-4**)*?*

Acts 19.1-7

The first verse takes up the story of Paul where **18.**23 left off, and brings him to Ephesus. His work there falls into the following categories: (*i*) as apostle (1-7); (*ii*) as apologist (8-10); (*iii*) as miracle-worker (11-20).

The disciples who professed to be ignorant of the Holy Spirit (2) must have been Gentiles if we take their statement in a precisely literal way, for all Jews would recall the Old Testament teaching of Psalm **51.**11; Isa. **63.**10, *etc.* These men were believers (2) and had been baptized as disciples of John the Baptist (3). Possibly the description "disciples" (1) is meant to fit this case, as in Matt. **14.**12, though it is just conceivable that they were disciples of Apollos, whose earlier life as an incomplete believer seems to have matched theirs (**18.**25). At all events we are clearly meant to see here: (*i*) An exceptional circumstance of a small (hence the number is given, 7) group of men who had believed in Christ (as the coming One, heralded by John) and had received a pre-Pentecostal baptism in anticipation of Messiah's coming. Their Christian knowledge and experience therefore, while sincere and genuine, was defective. (*ii*) A transition from the anticipatory baptism of John (and Apollos?) to the fulfilment—baptism which is the norm in the Gospel age. In Eph. **1.**13 Paul states explicitly the accepted sequence, with the same aorist participle in the Greek ("having believed") to be construed as coincident in time with the action of the chief verb. So, "Did you receive the Holy Spirit at the time of your believing?" corresponds exactly to the Pauline teaching: "At the time of your believing you were sealed with the promised Holy Spirit". No interval is envisaged, and the possibility of believing without the sealing of the Spirit is not entertained. This is why the Ephesian disciples are an exceptional case. (*iii*) A polemic against remaining content with John's baptism and a pre-Pentecostal faith and experience. The men were encouraged to submit to *Christian baptism*, which was followed by apostolic ordination and the gift of "tongues" (6).

Notes: V. 1: the wording implies that Paul's attention was drawn to these men and their needs. Hence his query (2). Vs. 2,3: the intimate connection between baptism and the gift of the Holy Spirit is plain (**2.**38; 1 Cor. **12.**13). John's baptism is described in **1.**5; **11.**16; **13.**24*f.*; **18.**25, and John's Gospel, **3.**23*ff.* A Johannine movement persisted in the later centuries.
Question: Is it possible to be a pre-Pentecostal believer today?

Acts 19.8-20

Paul's Ephesian ministry took on some features which are now familiar from our earlier readings. A ministry in the Jewish synagogue met with opposition and defamation (8,9), which obliged him to continue on neutral ground. The lecture-hall of Tyrannus is the new meeting-point, made available to Paul during the hot afternoon hours from 11 a.m. to 4 p.m. (a credible addition, supplied by the Western text, printed in R.S.V. margin) when the room would be unused. The townspeople would then be enjoying their midday siesta, while Paul and his devoted followers met to present Christ's claims to any who cared to come.

Paul gained some notoriety as a worker of miracles (11). This reputation induced some itinerant Jewish magicians to capitalize on his success, and to try their hand at using the name of Jesus as a formula of exorcism (13).

The spiritual power released by the apostolic ministry had other beneficial effects (18-20), with a notable display of the Gospel's effectiveness to counter and overcome false religion. No price was too high to obtain release from the tyranny of bad religion and crippling superstition which plagued the first-century world of Hellenistic man—and still grips modern man in spite of his technocracy and sophistication.

Notes: V. 8: "the kingdom of God": not a very common theme in the epistles, but we may refer to 1 Thess. **2.**12; Rom. **14.**17, and Col. **1.**13. V. 9: "the Way", as at **9.**2, a name for the early believers who were committed to the way of life ruled by Jesus Christ. Tyrannus was evidently a professional lecturer who hired out his room during its unused hours. Vs. 9 and 11 tell us that Paul had a very full day! V. 12: these garments are described in trade terms and refer to items which Paul used in his manual work. V. 13: a surviving papyrus has a list of such exorcisms, including "I beseech you by Jesus the God of the Hebrews". V. 14: possibly "high priest" was a pretentious claim Sceva made for himself, not to be taken too seriously.

Questions: (*i*) *How did Paul use his leisure hours* (*9*)*? How do we?* (*ii*) "*the folly of second-hand religion*" (*13,15*). *Are we ever guilty of this sort of borrowed vocabulary?*

Acts 19.21-41

Vs. 21, 22 are an intimation of Paul's future plans, including the expression of his desire, which henceforward runs like a thread through the rest of the book of Acts, to visit the imperial city, Rome.

The evidence for opposition here is partly factual (like the story here of the riot in the amphitheatre), and partly inferential (*e.g.*, the hints of a terrible danger to his life in 1 Cor. **15.**32; 2 Cor. **1.**8-10 and, probably, Phil. **1.**30; **2.**17).

Paul's preaching (26), as in the report of his Athenian sermon (**17.**24,29), was seen as a danger to the silversmiths; and a second occasion of Demetrius' protest may very well have been a period of social anarchy and unrest, following the assassination of Junius Silanus in A.D.54. The murder of this proconsul of Asia at the instigation of Agrippina may possibly have been carried out by two men who afterwards stayed on in Asia to oversee the imperial business until a successor to Silanus was appointed. G. S. Duncan makes this interesting suggestion in his book on *St. Paul's Ephesian Ministry*, and so explains (*a*) the reference to proconsuls (plural) in verse 38; and (*b*) Paul's grave danger in which his Roman citizenship failed to protect him from the venom of the mob and the authorities.

In God's providence, however, the apostle was able to call upon local influential friends (31). A moderating voice was raised by the Ephesian "town-clerk" (35-40). Luke did not fail to note the irony of the situation (32), though it may have been an ugly scene for a time until reason prevailed (41).

Notes: Vs. 25,27: "business is business" was Demetrius' ruling motto. V. 29: the Ephesian theatre has been excavated; it seated 25,000 persons in its day. Gaius may not have been a Macedonian (so the textual authorities grant) in view of **20.**4, where he is called a man of Derbe. Possibly, however, there were two men of this common name. See comment on the later verse. V. 32: the Greek word translated "assembly" is the regular word for "church" (so 41). V. 35: the image of Artemis was supposed to have fallen (like a meteorite?) from the sky.

Acts 20.1-6

From Ephesus Paul's journeys took him to Macedonia and then to southern Greece. Later as he faced opposition he decided to return northwards and to sail from Neapolis, the port of Philippi (6), across the Aegean to Troas on his long trip to Jerusalem (3: "set sail for Syria").

In a section which deals with Paul's uneventful travels we shall do well to dig a little below the surface, for this *was* an important period in his life. His visit to Macedonia (1) evidently was the same as that spoken of in 2 Cor. **2.**12 when he halted at Troas where he had arranged to meet Titus. This was a critical period in his apostolic service, for he had been insulted at Corinth (2 Cor. **2.**5) and had written a "severe letter" to rebuke a factious minority in the church which had opposed his authority. But this letter was not composed easily, as 2 Cor. **2.**4 makes clear. At Troas he was anxious to receive news of the letter's effect.

Indeed, so concerned was he and sorry that Titus had failed to rendezvous with him at Troas that he crossed over into Macedonia (2 Cor. **7.**5-13). There good news awaited him as Titus arrived with the report that the Corinthian disturbance was over and the church had voted confidence in him. From Macedonia, he wrote *2 Corinthians*, therefore; and followed it up with a visit (2), when he composed the *Epistle to the Romans*, which was sent out from Corinth.

The return trip, through Macedonia to Troas, brought him a further stage on his eastward journey. It was a slow journey (compare v. 6 with **16.**11, 12), and meant a hurried "stop-over" at Miletus instead of a diversionary visit to Ephesus (**20.**16). Why was he in a hurry (16)?

Notes: V. 4: the names of Paul's travel companions are interesting. Sopater may be the same as Sosipater of Romans **16.**21. Aristarchus was mentioned earlier at **19.**29, while Gaius may be the Macedonian of that verse if we accept (with N.E.B.) the variant reading "the Doberian" instead of "Derbaean" (N.E.B. marg.). Doberus was a Macedonian town, near Philippi. Tychicus is well known in the later imprisonment epistles as Paul's courier; and Trophimus recurs as the sick man of 2 Tim. **4.20**. V. 6: Passover days numbered a week, and probably a date in April A.D.57 is intended.

Acts 20.7-16

Vs. 7-12 are a description of the New Testament church at worship, and help to fill a gap in our knowledge of what went on when the early believers met in congregational assembly. Significant aspects: (*i*) the day is "the first day of the week"—*i.e.*, our Sunday (if, as is likely, Luke is using the Roman, not Jewish, calculation of the days of the week; *cf.* N.E.B.). This day became known as the Lord's day (Rev. **1.**10) in commemoration of His resurrection (Luke **24.**1; John **20.**19,26) and in contrast to the Jewish sabbath. Another feature of the Christians' holy day is given in 1 Cor. **16.**2. (*ii*) The time of this gathering at Troas is evidently evening ("he prolonged his speech until midnight" (7). (*iii*) The purpose is set out in the technical expression "to break bread" (7)—*i.e.*, to share a common meal which was held in order to observe a solemn remembrance of the Lord's death. The sense of this expression is given clearly in v. 11 and 1 Cor. **10.**16; and at this early stage of development, Christians observed a common meal (the *agape* or love-feast) in the framework of which there was a communion service (the Eucharist). This pattern seems clear from 1 Cor. **11.**17-34, and other Christian writings. (*iv*) In the context of this assembly Paul gave a "sermon" which was interrupted by Eutychus's unfortunate accident. An inland trip to Ephesus was not made because Paul had his eye on the calendar (16).

Notes: V. 7: "the morrow" refers to a new day, begun at "day-break" (11). Luke is therefore using the Roman system of reckoning, whose day was from midnight to midnight; not the Jewish, from sunset to sunset. V. 8: "lights" were torches which gave off heavy fumes. It is not surprising then that one young man nodded off (9) and fell down. V. 10: Paul acts like Elijah (1 Kings **17.**17*ff.*) and Elisha (2 Kings **4.** 34*f.*). V. 10: his "soul" (in O.T. sense of life's vital principle, *nephesh*) was still alive, although he was unconscious and concussed.

Acts 20.17-27

Opportunity to make contact with the Ephesian churches was not altogether lost; and if Paul couldn't come to them, they—or their leaders—could travel to meet him at Miletus. Ministers and church leaders should find special relevance and challenge in these words. Today's reading covers the first half of Paul's address, the only example of its kind in Acts as a speech delivered by him to a Christian community. "Almost certainly Luke heard it himself, and may even have taken shorthand notes" (F. F. Bruce). Certainly it carries all the marks of a Pauline composition.

Vs. 18-21 are mainly in the past, and relate Paul's type of ministry in Asia. This would be well known to his hearers, who, as "elders" (17) or "overseers" (28) would have special reason to be grateful for his "all-round" (20,21), if personally costly (19), ministry. "The plots of the Jews" (19) remind us of some far more serious danger to his life than Luke has recorded, as we observed earlier.

Vs. 22-27 are in the form of an announcement of what the future holds. Paul is on his way to Jerusalem, fully alive to the perils which beset him (22,23). In fact, he does not anticipate a return to Ephesus (25). His life is forfeit, yet expendable if only the divine purpose for which he was called and chosen may be realized (24). What was that purpose (**9.**15; **26.**16-18,22)? Was it achieved (2 Tim. **4.**6-8)?

Notes: V. 17: the "elders" are apparently to be equated with "guardians" (Gk. *episkopoi*, A.V., "overseers", 28), although the former may be the name of an office, the latter a function. V.19: *cf.* 1 Cor. **15.**32; 2 Cor. **1.** 8-10; **11.**23. V. 20: relevant to the pastoral office: "in public", and privately in the people's homes. Equally the two themes (21) still need strong emphasis. V. 22: "under the constraint of the (Holy) Spirit". V. 23: by inward monition or through the guidance of prophets like Agabus (**21.**11). Vs. 24,25: testifying to the Gospel and preaching the kingdom—are one and the same activity. V. 26: like Ezekiel's watchman (Ezek. **33.**1-6).

Meditation: Consider Paul's fidelity to his ministerial tasks.

Acts 20.28-38

Vs. 28-35 are the concluding part of this pastoral charge, in which exhortation and example meet and mingle. Paul's encouragements are given in such verses as 28,31,35. He holds himself up as a model to emulate in verses like 31,33,34. The call to vigilance and faithfulness is made all the more insistent and urgent because of the attacks of heretical teachers (29, 30) whose influence in the later church became only too apparent (*cf.* 1 Tim. **4.** 1-3; Jude; 2 Pet **2.**1-22; 1 John **4.** 1-6; Rev. **2.**2 in particular). The saddest warning is given in the announcement that these men will arise "from among your own selves"—*i.e.*, they will be apostate teachers who desert the Church's faith and introduce some distortion of Christian doctrine and ethics. Can you think of some modern counterpart to this "false teaching"?

Vs. 36-38. The elders escorted him to the quayside—the place of many tender farewells.

Notes: V. 28: the Church as a flock (John **10**) has a natural complement of its leaders as "overseers" (*episkopoi*) whose job it is to tend it and to protect it from marauding wolves (29). The Holy Spirit appoints such pastoral leaders over the Church, purchased (as Israel of old, Psa. **74.**2; Ex. **15.**16) by the blood of God's only Son (R.S.V. margin gives the best sense in the light of Jesus' relationship to God as His well-beloved, *cf.* Gen. **22.**2; Rom. **8.**32). V. 29: heretical leaders are often likened to wolves (Matt. **7.**15). V. 33: Samuel made a similar protest of disinterested concern (1 Sam. **12.**3). V. 34: "these hands"—one can almost *see* Paul point to his toil-worn hands as he spoke. The two words are in an emphatic place in the sentence. V. 35: a saying of Jesus not recorded in the Gospels, but evidently widely known. This suggests that a collection of His teaching was already in circulation among the churches.

Thought: The elders are to be built up (32) so that they may defend and tend the flock. The measure of one is the key to the other.

Acts 21.1-14

Vs. 1-6 narrate a further stage in the apostolic sea voyage from Miletus to Tyre. *En route* they called at various ports of call (1-3) until they reached Tyre on the Syrian coast. There a lengthy process of unloading the ship's cargo meant some delay (4), but Paul redeemed the time by making the acquaintance of Christian friends at Tyre. The church was formed there probably as a result of the missionary dispersal of **11.**19. A warning came to Paul, possibly by some inspired utterance in the church assembly, that he should not proceed to Jerusalem (4b); but he recognized some higher constraint (**20.**22) impelling him onwards. The cameo picture (5, 6) is a most touching scene, filled with tenderness and pathos. The final parting came as the two groups of Christians went their own ways: "*we* went on board the ship . . . *they* returned home". Many a missionary's valediction today is like this!

Vs. 7-14 take up again the theme of prophetic warnings given to Paul. This time it is Agabus—a noted prophet in the Judean churches

(**11**.27,28). Both Paul's companions and the Caesarean church sensed the imminent danger, and Paul's refusal to follow their advice was not made lightly or in a foolhardy manner (13). Like his Master, he was answerable to the divine will of which he had an assurance (Luke **13**.31-33). The church eventually accepted his firm persuasion (14) of God's will with a note of concurrence.

Notes: V. 1: lit., "we tore ourselves away from them". V. 7: the sea voyage ended at Ptolemais, the Roman port of Palestine, and thence Paul proceeded to Caesarea by road. V. 8: Philip and his family had settled at Caesarea (**8**.40). His unmarried daughters had the spiritual gift of 1 Corinthians **11**.5; **14**.3. V. 10: if we translate the time-phrase literally, with J. A. Findlay, it will mean "we stayed there more days (than we intended)". Perhaps it was congenial company or profitable discussion which detained the Pauline party; certainly Luke would benefit from the extra 'stop-over' by assembling materials for his literary works. V. 11: Agabus performs a symbolic action, like that of O.T. prophets, to lend extra force to his spoken message. V. 13: lit. "bleaching my heart by pounding it like a washerwoman" (Findlay) —a vivid metaphor in Paul's verb.

*Question : Both Paul and his Christian friends claimed the Spirit's guidance (**20**.22; **21**.4,11), yet reached opposite conclusions. What do we learn from this?*

Acts 21.15-26

James, the Lord's brother and leader of the Jerusalem church, gave the apostolic travellers a cautious welcome (18*ff.*). Their response to Paul's celebration of the Gospel and its success among the Gentile peoples (19) matched his enthusiasm with a sobering reflection that his ministry had been a source of embarrassment, partly based on a false report (21) and partly caused by the logical conclusion of Paul's doctrine of salvation by faith alone.

"What then is to be done?" was a natural question, demanding some action (22) to allay Jewish suspicions that Paul was advocating a wholesale rejection of the Jewish law and its relevance to Jews who became Christians. Underlying the fear of the Jewish party was undoubtedly a healthy regard for moral standards, and the insinuation that the Pauline message led inevitably to antinomianism— *i.e.*, a casting-off of all moral restraints in the interests of a supposed freedom and championing of divine grace (as in Rom. **6**.1*ff.*; Gal. **5**.13)— which dogged Paul all his life.

In fact, Paul had never quarrelled with the use of the Law for Jewish believers (see Rom. **2.**25; **3.**1*ff.*, 31; **7.**12) and had never renounced his Jewish heritage (1 Cor. **7.**18, **9.**20; 2 Cor. **11.**21*ff.*). It was an attempt to shackle *Gentile* converts with the Law which called forth his loudest protest, as in *Galatians*, which was written directly to a Gentile-Christian church in a controversial situation.

The evidence for his deep loyalty to his ancestry was provided by his acceptance of a Nazirite vow, both for himself and four men whose expenses—eight pigeons and two lambs in all (referred to in v. 24)—he paid. He is reminded of the earlier apostolic decree, made binding on the Gentile churches; and since this code (see on Acts **15**) did not infringe Gentile liberty in Christ, he was willing to comply (26).

Notes: V. 16: Mnason is called "an early disciple"—*i.e.*, a foundation-member of the church since its beginnings. V. 19: "he related ... the things God had done among the Gentiles"—as on a previous occasion (**15.**3*f.*, 12). V. 20: a true report of what was said, but was the statement exaggerated? V. 21: "the customs" are ethical standards. Hence the suggestion that Paul was leading people astray. V. 23: Paul had taken such a vow earlier (**18.**18). He had no need to purify himself from defilement (24), but conceded the point (26) out of deference to the elders. 1 Corinthians **9.**19-23 is well illustrated.

Thought: Two powerful ideas dominate Paul's thinking and action: the freedom of the Gospel, and the unity of the Church. Consider these in the light of today.

Acts 21.27-39

There is an indirect element of pathos in today's passage. Paul was arrested (33), and as far as the story in Acts goes, he was never again a free man! Verses 27-32 therefore tell of the apostle's last days of freedom.

Vs. 27-32. Paul's fulfilment of the vow in company with four Jewish Christians (23,24) was done openly—to serve as a notification of his ancestral loyalty. But he paid a heavy price for such notoriety. Certain Asian Jews spotted Trophimus, a Gentile from Ephesus, in his company, and drew the conclusion that Paul had taken him into the most sacred and restricted part of the Temple. This was a serious breach; hence the outcry (28). The gates were shut (by the Temple police chief presumably, 30c: he is referred to at **4.**1) to prevent further trouble; and the Roman tribune took Paul into protective custody (32,33).

Vs. 33-39. The fury of the crowd is seen both in their uncontrolled demonstration (34) and their determination to get at Paul, who was carried into the safety of the barracks on the backs of Roman soldiers (35).

Claudius Lysias (**23.**26) was the tribune's name. He thought that he had carried off a notable prisoner (38); and before the incident closed, Paul was given a chance to speak to the angry mob. But to no avail' (**22.**22, 23).

Notes: V. 27: the seven days of the Nazirite vow (Num. **6.**9*f.*) are meant. V. 28: the Romans honoured Jewish scruples about the sanctity of the Temple; a "middle wall of partition" (Eph. **2.**14) separated the Court of the Gentiles from the Court of Women and the Inner Court to which no Gentile could come. The penalty was death. Asian Jews had already proved (**20.**19) that they meant business in their enmity to the apostle of the Gentiles. V. 38: "the Egyptian" was evidently a man with a police record and wanted for his part in a Jerusalem uprising, quelled by Roman soldiers in A.D. 54 (Josephus tells us the story, and Klausner identified him with a false prophet named Ben Stada). He led the "Assassins" (lit. dagger-men). V. 39: Paul speaks up, giving his identity.

Acts 21.40—22.21

Paul's speech from the steps (40) was given to a quietened audience. The reason for this dramatic change which turned a restless, turbulent mob into a subdued body of listeners is found at **21.**40 and **22.**2. Speaking in Aramaic, Paul, with great tact, gained his audience's attention while he presented his "apology" (1) for his faith in Christ Jesus.

It falls into three parts: (*i*) his conduct before conversion (3-5); (*ii*) the circumstances of his conversion (6-14); (*iii*) his commission at conversion (15-21).

Paul adopts a frankly autobiographical pose, recalling his past life in the same way as in Gal. **1.**13-17; Phil. **3.**4-11, and 1 Tim. **1.**12-16. Confining our attention to the record in Acts, we note how Paul's pre-Christian life was seen from different points of view. The revered Jewish teacher Gamaliel (*cf.* **5.**34) no doubt saw in Saul of Tarsus an apt pupil, known for his zeal (3; Rom. **10.**2 puts this ardour in its true light). The early Christians saw in him a notorious enemy and persecutor, greatly to be feared, and the embodiment of undying hatred (4,5). Paul's own estimate of his former way of life is contained in the hints of (*a*) his diligence as Gamaliel's pupil, and (*b*) his all-consuming zeal for what he then believed to be God's honour.

Vs. 6-21. The circumstances of Paul's conversion are set in three different scenes: (*a*) on the road (6-11), where the living Jesus met him, captured his will, and claimed him as His servant. Note the new features recorded here, supplementary to the account in **9.**3-9. (*b*) In the house (12-16), identified earlier as Judas' home in Straight Street (**9.**11). (*c*) In the Temple (17-21). From this revealing piece of autobiography we can see the tremendous impression Stephen's martyrdom made on him (20), and Paul's appointment as apostle to the Gentile world was confirmed (21; Gal. **2.**7-9).

Notes: V. 14: "the Just One" = the Messiah (**3.**14). V. 15: his witness was grounded in personal experience, which no one could deny to him (*cf.* **26.**16). V. 16: Paul's baptism followed his conversion, imparting an assurance of forgiveness as he called on His name (**2.**21,38).
Meditation on Paul's conversion:
>Nay, but I yield, I yield,
>I can hold out no more;
>I sink by dying love compelled,
>And own Thee Conqueror.

Acts 22.22-29

The trance-vision in the Temple is of some importance both in its immediate impact on Paul (perhaps 2 Cor. **12.**2-4 refers to the experience; more likely 1 Cor. **9.**1 seems to indicate this occasion, when he *saw* the Lord) and its bearing on his future service. The commissioning word was "I will send you far away to the *Gentiles*" (21). The Roman tribune, evidently mystified over a speech (in a language foreign to him) which produced such a violent result (23), determined to get at the root of the matter, even if it meant torture (24,25). Paul appealed to his civil rights, and used his Roman citizenship to extricate himself from further indignity and suffering. He had no love of pain for its own sake – contrast with some of the later martyrs (*e.g.*, Ignatius) who took positive delight in their prospective sufferings.

The issue of verses 26-29 turns on Paul's possession of Roman citizenship, gained by inheritance from his parents (28). This automatically exempted him from such torture as the tribune intended to apply—a cruel method of "third degree" to extract a confession of guilt (24). The Roman soldier was amazed that a man like Paul could have afforded to buy his citizenship (27,28); but accepted the explanation that he gave.

Notes: V. 23: the offending thought was that Paul was claiming a divine commission to offer God's salvation *directly* to the Gentiles—*i.e.*, without requiring them to become Jews first or to become subservient to Jews (as in Isa. **61**.5). Throwing dust into the air, along with tearing clothes, is a sign of horror at blasphemy (Job **2**.12). V. 25: as at **16**.38, Paul reminds the Romans of his right to a fair trial. The flagrant mistake was that they had dared to bind him "uncondemned"—*re incognita:* without investigating his case—and were ready to flog him (from which he was, even if guilty, exempt). V. 28: the venerable Bede preserves an interesting reading: "It is easy to *say* you are a Roman citizen: I know how much it cost me!" In other words, the tribune speaks ironically, and marvels that such an undistinguished fellow as Paul could be a Roman. But appearances are often deceptive.

Acts 22.30—23.10

The Roman tribune's curiosity was further stimulated by the remarkable prisoner he had taken into custody. He was a man who knew his privilege as a Roman citizen to a trial (25,29), and at the same time had acquired a reputation as a trouble-maker among his own people (30). The simplest procedure, Claudius Lysias thought, was to bring accusers and accused together. So Paul was placed before the Jewish Sanhedrin (1).

Evidently Paul's protest divided the council, and Sir William Ramsay even suggests that, at verse 6, the Pharisees in the Sanhedrin walked across to take their place by the prisoner's side, as if to associate themselves with him. At all events two things stand out in the sequel: (*i*) Paul henceforth addresses the Pharisees by appealing to a doctrine which they and he as a Christian shared—the resurrection of the dead (denied by Sadducees, the high-priestly party, **4**.1,2; Mark **12**.18, *etc.*), and in response he gains the approval of this part of the Jewish legislature (9). (*ii*) In the subsequent outworking of his relations with the Jewish leaders, his main enemies are the Sadducees (**23**.14).

Notes: V. 1: see **26**.9; Phil. **3**.6. V. 2: Ananias is known to history as an unscrupulous ecclesiastical politician who held office and wielded influence for a long time. He was finally assassinated in A.D.66. by the nationalist terrorists referred to in **21.**38 Vs. 3, 5: Paul's retort seems to mean, "I couldn't recognize the high priest in the outrageous behaviour and speech of such a man as that!" The quotation from Exod. **22.**28, however, is half-apologetic. V. 3 reflects Matt. **23.**27, which confirms the view given above. The high priest may have worn the clothes of his office, but his spirit was *not* that of God's servant and leader of the people. V. 9: the Pharisees show, as at earlier times, a readiness to accept the message (**5.**34-40, **15.**5, **21.**20). The Sadducees, as at the trial and condemnation of Jesus, are the inveterate enemies.

Questions: Is the test of verse 9 valid today? How may a claim to fresh revelation and new truth be judged?

Acts 23.11-22

V. 11. Paul must have wondered what the issue would be. His life seemed to hang on a fragile thread, with three serious attempts made upon it in two days (**21.**31, **22.**22, **23.**10); "often near death" (2 Cor. **11.**23) was no poetic expression! The Lord's encouragement was, therefore, timely and to the point.

Vs. 12-15 give the "inside" story of a plot to put Paul out of the way once and for good. Fanatical Jews had made this compact to kill him. They had taken an oath on the matter (14), and sought the ready co-operation of the religious authority (15).

Vs. 16-22. The conspiracy was discovered by Paul's nephew— one of the rare sidelights on his family connections. The following scene, set in the Roman garrison-house, is a drama of suspense and mystery, with hurried exchanges of information, quick decisions, and sworn secrecy (22). The name of God doesn't appear in the swift-flowing narrative; no moral is drawn from the drama, and the characters act and speak like "men of the world" who might be found in any modern spy tale. The Bible doesn't moralize unnecessarily, nor is it tediously "pious" (as though every character in its story is constantly talking about religion). Yet the undertone of divine providence runs throughout; and God is *there*, if unseen and unrecognised, in the plans and counter-plans of enemies and friends. Of which Old Testament book does all this remind you?

Notes: V. 11: "take courage"—the Greek word is that used of Jesus' concern for His disciples' needs, in the Gospels (*e.g.*, Mark **6.**50). Paul's own desire to visit Rome (**19.**21; Rom. **1.**10,11) blends

with the Lord's will for His servant. Such a combination has irresistible force (Psa. **37.**4, 5). V. 12: abstinence from food and drink was a mark of earnestness in carrying out a purpose. Evil men can be thorough-going in their designs and often display a zeal which shames the Christian's half-heartedness (see, for illustration, Luke **16.**1-9). V. 18: "Paul the prisoner"—a state in which he later rejoiced to be (Eph. **3.**1; **4.**1; Col. **1.**24).
Thought: "All who take the sword will perish by the sword" (Matt. **26.**52). The irony is that the assassins whom Ananias abetted (14-16) ten years later claimed him as a victim.

Acts 23.23-35

The counter-plan, devised to foil the conspiracy of murder, was to abduct Paul by night from Jerusalem to Caesarea (23,24). A formidable bodyguard of foot soldiers, cavalry, and light-armed troops was detailed to escort the prisoner on the way to Felix, the Roman procurator at Caesarea, the headquarters of Roman authority in Palestine.

Lysias wrote a covering letter (26-30). The commentators, impressed by the realistic style of writing, wonder if Luke had actually seen a copy of this letter. Certainly it bears the imprint of what a Roman official may well say in such circumstances, including a touch of embellishment (27) designed to enhance *his* own reputation for prompt and decisive action. Strictly, Lysias did not learn of Paul's Roman status until later than the time of the arrest, and his motive in rescuing Paul was hardly that of verse 27! He tactfully omits an incident which had clearly embarrassed him (**22.**24-26)!

The apostle was ushered into the presence of Felix, whose predecessor in the governor's office—Pilate—is well known. Felix's term began in A.D.52, and was marked with uprisings and fierce countermeasures. As a result of one such commotion and its harsh treatment by Felix (**24.**27), he was recalled. A contemporary historian sums up his character: "He exercised the power of a king with the mind of a slave". Luke is more kindly in his record (especially **24.**22,23), but picks out some basic flaws in his character (**24.**26,27).

Notes: V. 23: about 9.30 p.m. From the size of the escort, it is clear that Lysias was taking no more chances. Contrast Ezra **8.**22. V. 24: the plural "mounts" (horses or mules) implies that Paul had his friends, including Luke, with him—*cf.* **24.**23. V. 26: a title of respect, also given to Luke's first reader (Luke **1.**3). V. 34: a similar question, put for purposes of identification, was asked concerning the Lord at His trial (Luke 23.6, 7). V. 35: Paul spent two years at the official residence of the governor, built by Herod the Great; hence the name.

To think over: Our letter-writing is a revelation of character. How does Lysias' character shine through his letter to Felix?

Acts 24.1-9

In today's reading we see Paul through the eyes of his enemies (particularly 5), and learn something of how the earliest Christians had to contend with misrepresentation and implacable hate.

"The speech of Tertullus is a delightful parody of the oratory of the second-rate Greek hired pleader; Luke must have enjoyed writing it. It begins with a high-flown compliment, and then quite suddenly subsides into the baldest colloquialism, as if the poor creature could not keep it up" (Findlay).

Tertullus's rhetoric leads him into (*i*) culpable exaggeration (2, "much peace" is sharply contradicted by the series of uprisings and punitive retaliations which had disgraced Felix's tenure of office); (*ii*) a distortion of the facts (5, which tried to denigrate Paul by making him no better than a Messianic revolutionary, like the man of 21.38, whom Felix, aided by Jews, had put down); and (*iii*) a perverted sense of justice (7, which is relegated to the R.S.V. margin, but many editors believe it to be authentic). Clearly something more needs to be added to explain the reason for Paul's "arrest" by the Jews. Notice the slant which Tertullus gives to the recent events, silently glossing over any thought that the Jews were ready to lynch their enemy, and putting the blame for "violence" on Lysias' head (7). His hint ("we would have judged him according to our law", 6) may suggest that there was no need for Felix to bother himself overmuch with this case —let him just release Paul, for them to deal with!

Notes: V. 4: "briefly"—at least one redeeming feature of the speech, and he kept to his promise. V. 5: a threefold charge is brought against Paul. He is accused of being (*i*) a troublesome pest—*i.e.*, a seditious agitator against the Roman authority; this was designed to get Felix's interest: (*ii*) a ringleader of Nazarenes—*i.e.*, a heretical Jewish sect, based on the teaching of an executed false prophet: (*iii*) an attempted violator of the Temple, whose claim to sanctity the Romans respected. How much was (*i*) true? (*ii*) false? (*iii*) distorted? V. 7: *cf.* John 18.31. *Thought:* Read again the account of Paul's encounter with the Jews (**21.27**_ff._). Both Claudius Lysias (**23.26**_ff._) and Tertullus (**24.2**_ff._) have given their own—different—versions of it. Shall we turn this thought into prayer for all who influence public opinion in our newspapers, radio, and TV, that _facts_ may be clearly distinguished from _comment_.

Acts 24.10-21

The defence which Paul makes before the governor's tribunal deals point by point with the accusations levelled against him. The main intention, however, is to show that he is innocent of all _political_ charges, and that the real issue between him and the Jews is a _theological_ one (20,21). We may take up the individual rebuttals he makes to the list of accusations which faced him: (_i_) Paul's visit to Jerusalem was a recent happening and the facts of the case should be known to all (11); (_ii_) he denied all responsibility as a trouble-maker at that time. He was going about his lawful occasions (12,18); (_iii_) in any case, the men who confronted him at Felix's palace were not the same as the real assailants (13,18b,19: "Jews from Asia" were the disturbers of the peace); (_iv_) The nub of the dispute between Paul and the Jews who supported Tertullus' castigation (5,9) was found in a conflicting interpretation of Scripture (14,15) and a debate over theology (21). The implication which Paul intended is clear: he himself had a clear conscience over the charges of supposed agitation (16) and the matter before the governor had no political significance. The "one thing" was a domestic affair which ought to be settled peacefully.

In the course of this brief statement Paul has indirectly made his position clear. He was and always had been—a loyal Israelite (14) with a faith built on the Old Testament revelation which, as prophetic Scripture, looks beyond itself to the fulfilment of divine promises. Part of that faith is an expectation of resurrection (15,21)—a Pharisaic tenet also. From this belief it is an easy step to the central _Christian_ article of faith: the resurrection of Jesus, which validated His Messiahship as Israel's King and Saviour. Paul is no iconoclast, with a relish for acting irresponsibly and upturning his ancestral beliefs (16). In fact, the opposite is true. He had come to Jerusalem with money for _Jewish_-Christians, as a token of charitable concern and a proof of unity among the one people of God (17).
Notes: V. 14: non-Christians may call them a "sect" (_i.e._, heterodox party within the Jewish fold), but the correct title was "the Way",

9.2; **19.**9,23; **22.**4; **24.**22). The qualification "God *of our fathers*" is important. Like Moses (Ex. **3.**13) and the prophets of Israel (Hos. **12.**9,13; **13.**4,5; Amos **2.**10, *etc.*) Paul harks back to God's earlier revelation, at the same time pointing forward to its future consummation. V. 17: the collection for the saints occupied much of his time and attention (2 Cor. **8**–**9**; Rom. **15.**25*ff.*).

Acts 24.22-27

Felix was in no mind to settle the dispute there and then, and deferred the case (22,23). One notable interview which brought the two men together is described (24,25). Felix's intention was clear; he wanted to hear the Christian missionary speak on a vital theme. (What could have been more congenial to Paul than to expound "faith in Christ Jesus"?) Paul, however, refused to fawn on his distinguished audience and to ingratiate himself with those who had the power to set him free. The trio of "justice" (better "righteousness", in the sense of Romans **1**—**4**, as a divine standard by which human life is tested and condemned and a divine offer in the Gospel), "self-control" and "future judgment" was hardly calculated to make the preacher popular. It formed "the very subjects that Felix and Drusilla most needed to hear about" (F. F. Bruce), but not what they *wanted* to be reminded of, as is apparent from their known characters at that time. Small wonder, then, that Felix was terrified, and cut short the interview on that occasion. Paul, however, was given further opportunities (26b), but evidently without making much of a deep impression upon this interested dilettante. At least, he saw no injustice in holding in detention a blameless man (27). So much for his religious interest!

Notes: V. 22: apparently Lysias never came, or else this was Felix's way of postponing proceedings and the verdict *sine die*. Paul had no redress and no choice but to hope for a discharge. When this became unlikely, he played a trump card (**25.**11). V. 23: the Roman term for this detention *libera custodia* ("free custody") shows that it was not irksome, but Paul must have wondered why, in God's providence, his active ministry was curtailed. V. 24: Drusilla had been enticed away from her husband, Aziz, by Felix and persuaded to join his *harem* as his third, polygamous wife. V. 26: Paul's financial state gives the mark of some affluence at this time of his life (implied in **21.**24 and **28.**30).

Meditations: (*i*) *Two men's consciences are dramatically sounded: Paul's* (16) *and Felix's* (25). (*ii*) *"When I have some spare time I'll send for you"* (25). *Does "spare-time religion" ever satisfy?*

Acts 25.1-12

Festus succeeded to the office of procurator at Caesarea in A.D.58. Little is known of him—in fact, virtually nothing apart from what Luke and the Jewish historian Josephus tell us.

Paul's fortunes seem to be unchanged. The Roman authorities were unwilling to decide his case; one motive for such tardiness is given in **24.27**. The next scene is fraught with momentous consequences. A second deputation of Jews, sent from Jerusalem, had nothing new to say and repeated the unfounded charges as on the former occasion (7). Paul simply denied any complicity (8). Then came the decision-laden question: "Do you wish to go up to Jerusalem?" (9). The prisoner was clearly at the crossroads. If he said yes, he would play himself nicely into the hands of his accusers, perhaps admitting that there was a case to answer and that they were competent to act in this matter. Besides, his safety was involved, and he must have known something of the attempt which was planned on his life (3). On the other side, to refuse now might alienate Festus and lose the protection of Roman custody.

Paul gave a deliberate reply, probably using the technical phrase to which he was entitled as a citizen of the empire: *Caesarem appello*— "I appeal to Caesar" (11). This exercise of his privilege at once quashed all local proceedings, and transferred his case to the imperial court of Nero in Rome, as Festus perceived (12). So, in a roundabout way, the divine purpose was strangely carried forward (**23.11**).

Notes: Vs. 3,9: Festus, having been asked this favour, grants it. His motto seems to have been "Anything for a quiet life". Considerations of justice and fair play don't seem to have weighed much. Herod Agrippa is more forthright (**26.31**). V. 8: "against Caesar"; this shows that the Jews were accusing him of a political offence. V. 11: a final plea of innocence, implying that there were no charges to answer. The appeal to Caesar indicates that Paul had despaired of any justice at such a crooked court where a plaintiff's "favour" influences the presiding judge on the tribunal seat (3,9).
Today's prayer: For all who make and administer our laws.

Acts 25.13-27

Vs. 13-22: Agrippa visits Festus. Herod Agrippa II was a political figure, important as a tetrarch of some districts in north Palestine, and also as the secular head of the Jewish church who appointed the high priesthood. He was a character of some influence, therefore.

A state visit of Herod, along with his sister Bernice, gave Festus a chance to mention Paul's case (13,14). This was not to re-try him (which was now beyond his power, since Paul had appealed directly to the emperor), but simply to get Herod's views and thereby to have information for the dossier to be sent to the imperial court. One cardinal Christian truth had penetrated into his mind (19), which proves that the general debate over the resurrection of the dead (24.15,21) turned upon the case of *one* particular resurrection—*viz.*, that of the Messiah. This special application of a principle was more than the Pharisees could allow or believe; but at least the pagan Roman had the wit to see what Paul was continually talking about.

Vs. 23-27. Luke was evidently in close touch with these proceedings, as his detailed descriptions show (23).

Notes: V. 13: Herod Agrippa and Bernice were related, but rumour darkly hinted at their immoral ways. V. 19: "superstition"; the Greek word may carry a neutral sense, "religion", as well as a derogatory one, as R.S.V. gives. Festus, perhaps unwittingly, goes to the heart of the matter. The tenses of the verbs he uses are interesting: one Jesus Who *has been dead* (for some time), Whom Paul *was repeatedly saying* to be alive. V. 26: "examined"—*i.e.*, by this enquiry. This would provide information to send off to "my Lord" = the emperor, concerning the prisoner.

Exercise: Look back over the previous chapters, and notice the fundamental importance of the resurrection of Jesus both as a central affirmation of faith and a living experience in the early Christians' fellowship and service.

Question: Do I know a living Christ today?

Acts 26.1-18

After a brief introduction (2,3), designed to pay deference to "King Agrippa", whose Jewish ancestry would give him a special sympathy with Paul's case, the apostle opens up his "defence" in the three main sections of our portion.

(*i*) The story of his past life (4-11). This may be summed up as "sincere, but wrong", with verse 9 as its epitome. Yet, in a strange way, the Christians were simply announcing in Messiah's resurrection (8) a special application of a tenet cherished by all good Pharisees (6,7).

(*ii*) The crisis of his conversion (12-15). His encounter with the living Lord was indeed a crisis—*i.e.*, a judgment upon his past life and a new beginning, memorably stated in 2 Cor. **4.**6; **5.**17 as a new creation. In the darkness of his ignorance and folly, the light of God had shone (13); and the real meaning of his persecuting zeal was made known (14,15), for in attacking His people, Saul was wounding Christ Himself—a fearful possibility which he never forgot (1 Cor. **8.**11-13) and which very probably became the basis of his teaching on the Church as Christ's body (see 1 Cor. **12.**12; Eph. **5.**23,29,30).

(*iii*) The terms of his commission (16-18). The account of what was said to him is here given in its fullest detail, and repays close study. The life-work of the future apostle to the Gentiles is admirably sketched, from the initial experience of personal knowledge of Christ (16, "in which you have seen me") to the establishing of Pauline churches (18: "those who are sanctified", 1 Cor. **1.**2, *etc.*). Notice the effect of Gospel ministry, which includes conversion, deliverance, forgiveness, and a place in the new society of Christ's people (18). All these benefits recur in Paul's writings.

Notes: Vs. 2,3: intended to put the speaker *en rapport* with his hearer, but not the flattery of **24.**2*ff.* V. 4: Paul's essentially Jewish upbringing and training in Jerusalem is important, as W. C. van Unnik has shown, to dispel the notion that Paul took over a Greek mystery religion and turned it into his version of Christianity! V. 7: "observe that Paul knew nothing of the fiction of the 'lost' tribes" (Bruce). V. 10: does this mean that Paul had been a member of the Sanhedrin—and therefore at one time a married man? V. 14: note the addition to **9.**4 of a proverbial line, reminding us that his zeal masked a disquieted conscience.

Meditation: Try to match the parts of verse 18 with the teaching of the epistles (e.g., Col. **1.**12-14).

Acts 26.19-32

When the facts are examined—Paul concluded—there is nothing anti-Jewish in the message he brought; rather, it complements and brings to fulfilment the Old Testament hope of a Messiah, humiliated yet vindicated and the author of God's blessings to all men, both the Jewish people and the Gentile races (22,23).

Festus was plainly out of his depth. Much study, the Preacher remarked, is a weariness of the flesh (Ecc. **12.**12); the Roman governor pronounced it a danger to sanity (24). Paul repelled that charge, insisting that his Christian knowledge and experience were based on the opposite of "madness"—*viz.*, soberness, the possession of a right mind (see 2 Cor. **5.**13 for the contrast). There is nothing irrational in Christianity in the sense of claims which are contrary to reason (*cf.* 8), although there is much that is *above* human reason, and may be known only by faith.

The interchange of conversation between Paul and Agrippa (26-29) is full of interest. The Christian preacher confidently appeals to what is public knowledge—thereby incidentally dispelling the latter-day idea that Christianity is wrapped in mists of obscurity and legend; and presses home the appeal (27). Agrippa eases himself off the horns of such a dilemma with a facetious retort: "In short, you are trying to persuade me to play the Christian". Paul picks up the king's words: "The short and the long of it is—I wish that you and all who hear me today could *become* (as opposed to "play a part") as I am—but not as a prisoner!"

Notes: V. 19: the vision is that mentioned in **22.**17*f.* which (as implied in 16-18) assured him of his call to be a missionary to the *Gentiles*. V. 22: Paul appeals, as elsewhere (Rom. **3.**21), to the united witness of the two major sections of the Jewish scriptures. V. 23: *cf.* Luke **24.**25*ff.*, 44. His resurrection is spoken of as a "first instalment" (1 Cor. **15.**20), guaranteeing that of all His people (2 Tim. **1.**10). V. 24: Festus speaks angrily with a loud voice; Paul's reply is restrained. V. 28: the best parallel is 1 Kings **21.**7: "Is it like this that you play a king's part in Israel?"

To ponder: Four characters are here: Bernice, Herod Agrippa, Festus, and Paul. How do they come out of this exchange of views and convictions?

Acts 27.1-12

Commentators praise the vividness and accuracy of this narrative which describes Paul's sea voyage from Palestine to Italy; it is "one of the most instructive documents for the knowledge of ancient seamanship". In this way Paul's long-cherished ambition to get to Rome is made good, though in circumstances (1) which he did not relish. And by this long journey the divine promise was realized (**23.**11).

Paul had travelling companions all the way; one of them is named (2) and at least one other was in the party—Luke the narrator (2; "*we* put to sea").

The Roman centurion Julius showed consideration to the Christian prisoner he had in custody, even to the extent of permitting him to make contact with his fellow-believers at Sidon. We should probably, however, understand verse 3 to mean: "allowed his friends to visit him" on board before they disembarked.

Having trans-shipped at Myra, the party sailed on a corn-ship bound for Italy. The next stage of the voyage was slow and difficult, owing to unfavourable winds and the need to negotiate dangerous coastal rocks.

At Fair Havens (8) Paul came forward with a suggestion. The inference is that the ship's captain should have anchored in the security of Fair Havens bay during the stormy season. Instead, with Paul's advice ignored (11), the decision of the ship's personnel was to sail on, hoping at all events to get to Phoenice (or Phoenix) and to winter there (12).

Notes: V. 1: there is evidence of the presence of this cohort in Syria in first-century A.D. V. 2: Aristarchus is found later as a companion of Paul's at Rome (Col.**4.**10; Philem. 24), and we may suppose that he travelled with him all the way. V. 9: "the fast" is the Day of Atonement, to be dated about the 5th October in that year. Ancient sailors regarded the 14th September as the beginning of a two-month period when all navigation was hazardous; so it was particularly risky to venture out of harbour in mid-October. Paul was overruled by the various officials—the helmsman and owner (11)—whose decision influenced the centurion.

Acts 27.13-32

Vs. 13-20. The sailors were deceived into thinking that a gentle southerly wind was a good augury (13). The ship put out from Fair Havens and coasted along the shore of Crete, only suddenly to be struck by the fearsome Euraquilo—a fierce north-easterly gale which, sweeping down from Mount Ida in Crete, quickly had the vessel out of control (15). The danger was that the strong waves would overwhelm the ship or smash her structure (hence the measure which was taken of undergirding the ship, 17); or else she would be driven helplessly on to the Syrtis, a dreadful whirlpool and quicksands off the North African coast.

Vs. 21-26. Paul's commanding position is evident. Not for the first time he had faced the perils of the storm (2 Cor. 11.26); and out of his past experience and present faith he speaks words of (*i*) cheer (22); (*ii*) explanation, giving grounds for his confidence and courage (23); and (*iii*) testimony (25). One man's presence and faith made all the difference.

Vs. 27-32. After two weeks of drifting at the mercy of the elements, the first signs were recognized that Paul's promise (26) was true. The sailors sensed that they were nearing shore as they took soundings (28) and possibly heard the sound of breakers on the shore. Anchors were dropped to brake the vessel (29); and Paul again showed his leadership in preventing a party of sailors from saving their own skins at the expense of the rest (30-32).

Notes: V. 17: the measures included passing a cable round the ship several times, pulling it taut, to ease the strain and prevent the timbers working loose and the seams opening (Findlay). V. 18: as in the scene of Jonah 1.5. V. 21: perhaps the food was sodden—or the mariners were seasick! Paul's remarks are a mild "I told you so". V. 24: *cf.* Gen. 18.26 for the principle that good men protect the community (Gen. 19.22).

Question: "*I have faith in God*" (*25*). *How did Paul's faith show itself in this critical situation?*

Acts 27.33-44

The apostle's leadership is again seen, and among a crew and passenger list of 276 men he stands out as a man of practical faith and sturdy common-sense (34). The angelic vision (23) and the divine promise of safety (24) were food enough for him, and he was prepared to act upon the assurance which had come to him (34b). With his splendid example to encourage them (35), the rest of the ship's complement took fresh heart (36).

The shipwreck scene is dramatically painted in the remaining verses of the chapter (39-44). The sailors severed the cables and left the anchors in the sea; at the same time unleashing the steering-paddles, and hoisting the foresail to catch a wind, they drove the ship on to the shore (40).

The beaching operation worked. The ship struck a spit of land which jutted out where the two seas met (41, R.S.V. marg.), and the prow became embedded in the sandbank of the promontory, while the stern was broken up by the force of the sea (41).

The soldiers' plan to kill off the prisoners lest they should escape in the confusion of the shipwreck was thwarted—for Paul's sake, to whom everyone owed a great deal. We can only guess by what method—swimming, clutching a plank, or holding part of the ship's spar—Paul and Luke reached land.

Notes: V. 34: the Greek term, elsewhere rendered "salvation", here means physical well-being (as in Phil. **1.**19). The next sentence is an O.T. proverb (1 Sam. **14.**45; 2 Sam. **14.**11; 1 Kings **1.**52; *cf.* Luke **21.** 18). V. 35: an acknowledgment of God's goodness in providing food, though the Western text adds that Paul shared this meal with "us" (presumably Luke and Aristarchus) and understands it as a sacramental meal (so Ramsay). V. 37: R.S.V. margin gives smaller numbers, but the figure of 276 is only half the complement of a ship on which Josephus travelled to Rome, so there is no inherent difficulty in the larger figure. V. 44: the Greek *may* mean :"some on the backs of members of the crew"—a vivid touch!

Acts 28.1-6

The island on which the storm-tossed sailors found refuge was Malta —a Phoenician word which, by a strange coincidence, means "escape". It has been suggested that Luke was aware of this correspondence when he wrote verse 1: "We recognized that the island deserved its name". Rain and cold added to the miseries of their experiences on board ship and then in the water; so the warmth of a fire (2) was especially appreciated, as the historian records.

The incident of the viper's sudden appearance from among the brushwood which Paul was helping to gather for the fire well illustrates popular opinion on the island. The first reaction was to see in the event a judgment on Paul the prisoner, recognized as such possibly by his dress, or perhaps by the chain he was still wearing. The viper, however, was shaken off his hand before it could harm him; and as no ill-effect followed, the Maltese changed their tune, and hailed him as a divinity, like the people of Lystra (**14.**11, 12). Such is the fickleness of human opinion, which oscillates with great ease between the two extremes of branding Paul a murderer and then of greeting him as a god come to earth. "The sudden reversal of opinion about Paul may be compared and contrasted with the attitude of the Lycaonians in **14.**11*ff.*, who first acclaimed him as a god, and later nearly stoned him to death" (Bruce).

Notes: V. 2: "natives": lit. barbarians, but not in the sense of uncivilized (which Maltese were not), but meaning "not speaking Greek". Their dialect was Phoenician, which sounded to Greek ears as *bar-bar*, a cacophony of strange words! None the less, Luke pays tribute to their hospitable welcome. V. 4: there is an ancient tale of a murderer who escaped from a storm at sea and was shipwrecked on the North African coast, where he died from a viper's sting. *Cf.* Amos 5.19. "Justice"—the Maltese natives associated Paul's predicament, with a snake hanging on to his hand, as a piece of Nemesis which had at length caught up with him.

Thought: "Hospitality is variously regarded as a 'fine art', a joyous privilege, an unwelcome necessity, or an opportunity for display. The New Testament writers emphasize its importance as a Christian grace and as a species of evangelistic service" (C. R. Erdman). Consider Rom. **12.**13; 1 *Tim.* **3.**2; *Tit.* **1.**8; *Heb.* **13.**2; *and* 1 *Pet.* **4.**9.

Acts 28.7-16

Vs. 7-10. "One good turn deserves another". On the one side, Publius extended to the apostle some friendly hospitality which lasted three days (7), and, on the other hand, he received the added happiness of seeing his father cured of gastric fever and dysentery, following the visit and prayer of Paul (8).

Paul's healing ministry became widely known, and sick folk throughout the island saw a chance to be healed by this Christian leader whom the ocean had washed up on to their beach. They showed their gratitude by the offer of gifts and ship's stores (10).

Luke doesn't comment on any deeper spiritual significance of these incidents: did Paul preach the Gospel as he exercised a ministry of prayer and healing? Were any Maltese won for Christ? Did the apostolic party leave behind a Christian community? The record is silent; but we may surely believe that here was an evangelistic opportunity too good to be missed.

Vs. 11-16. The Roman writer Pliny informs us that the winter season when the seas were closed for navigable traffic ended on February 7th; and we may infer that the three months' stay on the island ended about that time of the year (11). The ship in which they resumed their journey was another Alexandrian grain-ship which bore as a figure-head the "Heavenly Twins" (Castor and Pollux, the patron saints of navigators in the ancient world).

The course led them at last to Puteoli in the Bay of Naples. In this flourishing seaport a Christian fellowship was contacted, and Paul and his company had a week with them. The last "leg" of the long journey brought them *via* the Appian Way to within sight of the Imperial City.

Notes: V.7: "chief man of the island"—Luke's accuracy is confirmed by inscriptions which show that this was the title of the Roman governor. Paul's citizenship would be his passport to the governor's residence. V. 10: it could mean "paid us handsome fees" for the medical treatment received, as Luke the "dear doctor" (Col. **4.**14) may have observed. V. 15: Christian fellowship meant much to Paul, and he was obviously touched by this "welcome party" which came forty-three miles to greet him.

Question: God used Paul's ministrations to heal (8,9); but he worked no magical cure and was not always successful (2 Tim. **4.**20). Why?

Acts 28.17-30

Rome at last! The narrative moves to its zenith, as Bengel observed in his commentary written in the mid-eighteenth century: "The victory of the Word of God: Paul at Rome, the climax of the Gospel, the conclusion of Acts". Paul's attempt to put himself in the clear with Jewish leaders at Rome failed, although he was able to (*i*) make plain the reason for his being in Rome as a prisoner (17-20) and (*ii*) testify, at a conference called for the purpose, concerning "the hope of Israel" (20) and the central theme of the Gospel message (23).

As on so many previous occasions, his preaching divided men into two camps (24; *cf*. 1 Cor. **1.**18; 2 Cor. **2.**15,16). As the unconvinced Jews left in total disarray (25,29, R.S.V. marg.), Paul clinched his point with a quotation from the Old Testament and with a hint of his teaching, amplified and worked out in Romans **9—11**, that the Gentiles have received mercy because of the disobedience of Israel (Rom. **11.**30)—another leading *motif* in the preceding record of how the Gospel was brought from Jerusalem to Rome.

"They will listen" (28): this is the final thrust of the Pauline testimony. Israel's salvation, rejected by her national representatives and leaders, is now offered to the Gentiles, and nothing can stop the onward march of God's truth to the "uttermost part of the earth" (**1.**8, A. V., K.J.V.). Paul's "free custody" (as the Romans called it, 30,31) gave him opportunity to do the work of an evangelist among an audience which had free access to his hired room, which was his prison-cell; and the closing words "quite openly and unhindered" stress both his personal confidence (*cf*. Phil. **1.**20 for the same expression, "with full courage") and the unrestricted scope he enjoyed to proclaim the message of Christ.

These two elements—the preacher's boldness and an all-embracing proclamation—are interwoven in the fabric of the history of Acts as it speaks of the good news: "it began at Jerusalem; it finishes at Rome. Here, O Church, is your model. It is your duty to keep it and to guard your deposit" (Bengel).

Questions: (*i*) What do you understand by Paul's preaching of the kingdom of God (23,31) to his hearers? (*ii*) Trace the way (*a*) Israel refused the Gospel offer in Luke's story; and (*b*) the Gentiles received it.

Note:
These Bible Study Books normally offer a minimum of 92 readings, covering three months. In the present book, however, the author felt that the chapters most naturally divided into 91 sections, and it seemed unrealistic to insist on 92 readings. We are sure readers will understand this.